GOOD & CHEAP

ETHNIC EATS

UNDER $10

In and Around New York

GOOD & CHEAP
ETHNIC EATS
UNDER $10

In and Around New York

ROBERT
SIETSEMA

CITY & COMPANY
NEW YORK

City & Company
175 Fifth Avenue, Suite 2255
New York, NY 10010

Printed in the United States of America

Cover design by Iris Weinstein
Interior design by Sarah Durham

Library of Congress Cataloging-in-Publication Data:
Sietsema, Robert.
Good and cheap ethnic eats under $10 in and around New York /
by Robert Sietsema
p. cm.
Includes index.
ISBN 1-885492-05-7 : $9.95
1. Ethnic restaurants–New York (N.Y.)–Directories. 2. New York
(N.Y.)–Guidebooks. I. Title.
TX907.3.N72N483   1994
647.957471–dc20   94-26454
                                            CIP

First printing October 1994
10 9 8 7 6 5 4 3 2 1

ACKNOWLEDGMENTS

Many of the reviews in this book were originally published in *Down the Hatch*, a bimonthly food fanzine that I started in 1990. Also included are updated reviews of restaurants covered in my *Village Voice* column, "Counter Culture," plus a large number of new reviews written especially for the present volume.

I am grateful to Erica Marcus, the editor of this book, for organizing and preparing the material for publication. She also reviewed three of her favorite restaurants, which are designated by "(E.M.)" in the text. Thanks are due my publisher, Helene Silver, former *Village Voice* editor Amy Virshup, my agent Faith Hamlin, and the staff of *Down the Hatch*, W. Christopher Nelson, Gretchen Van Dyk, and Tracy Van Dyk.

CONTENTS

INTRODUCTION

I came to New York in 1977 from the Midwest, the land of meat loaf and mashed potatoes. The food of the city was a fantastic revelation: My first day in town found me at Katz's Deli on Houston Street scarfing pastrami sandwiches and Dr. Brown's Cel-Ray, and I never stopped eating. At that time, Japanese restaurants were the latest thing, and sushi was being offered for the first time. Falafel had taken the Village by storm, and there were only two Indian restaurants on East 6th Street (soon to be twenty). Shortly thereafter, Korean restaurants arrived in Midtown, open all night and with menus that had a hundred or so unrecognizable (to me, at least) entrées. I tried every variety of ethnic food I could get my hands on, and each day promised a new taste sensation.

Sometimes I worried that I'd run out of new things to try, that someday I'd open a menu and recognize every dish on it. Luckily, that day never arrived, because every time I got tired of one cuisine or another, a new immigrant group would hit town, open their unobtrusive restaurants, and begin serving the delectable foods that reminded them of home and that seemed to me like instant vacations to exotic parts of the world.

This book contains reviews of 94 restaurants, where you will find the food to be exotic, tasty, and inexpensive. Although it used to be my goal to eat for $5.00 or less, you will see from a few of the reviews in this book that my resolve has sadly lapsed. Still, nearly every meal mentioned falls within the $5.00 to $10.00 range. (Prices at these restaurants were accurate at press time, but even if they inflate, they will still be among the most reasonable in the city.)

Some words of warning and encouragement: The world of small ethnic eateries is a volatile one. Restaurants open and close daily. Even though the information here was verified at the time of publication, phone before you go to make sure the place is still in business. Or, if you're the impulsive sort, like me, just go. If you find your choice closed, scout around the neighborhood—ethnic restaurants tend to travel in packs, as in Flushing's Chinatown or the Colombian part of Jackson Heights. Once you've found a place, don't be deterred if you don't recognize the food or the staff doesn't speak your language. They'll probably enjoy trying their food out on you and noting your reaction. (Remember, you can always point to something that someone else is eating.)

I hope that this book will serve not only as a convenient advisory for good places to eat, but as a point of departure for your own culinary adventures. Remember, life is too short to have a bad meal.

ROBERT SIETSEMA

AFRICAN

The roots of African culture run very deep in America, but never in this century have there been so many actual Africans among us. Senegalese men selling watches is a common sight, as are cabdrivers from Nigeria and Ghana. It was inevitable that the new immigrants brought their food to this country, and just as inevitable that we should want to eat it.

Although the African restaurants in New York feature an abundance of meat, chicken, fresh seafood, and vegetables, the vast majority of people living in Africa see a piece of meat or chicken once a month or less and eat nothing but porridge of one sort or another. These porridges (often referred to as "mashes") take many forms. *Toa*, a millet porridge eaten in Burkina Faso (a small country in West Africa), is always served with a sauce made with tomatoes or dried okra. *Kenkey*, from Nigeria, is cornmeal mixed with water, hung up to ferment for a couple of weeks, and then steamed. *Fufu* is boiled cassava and potato flour that has been whipped into a rubbery, resilient consistency. It can also be made of plantains or yams. *Gari* is a mash made from cassava meal; *banku* is made from cornmeal.

After eating at one of the following restaurants, visit the West African Grocery at 40th Street and 9th Avenue, which sells an astounding assortment of African food products–dried fish, herbs and spices, even African beer. This is your best chance to meet African people on their own turf.

KORYOE RESTAURANT AND CAFE
Manhattan
3151 Broadway bet. Tiemann Pl. & Lasalle St.
(212) 316-2950
Subway stop: 125th St. on 1 or 9 train

A Ghanian cabdriver told me about two restaurants that feature the foods of West Africa. The first is Koryoe Restaurant and Cafe in Harlem. The menu describes the restaurant as "Specializing in food from Ghana, Nigeria, Ivory Coast, Togo, Guinea, Senegal, Sierra Leone and other African countries." The ten-item section called "Special African Dishes" lists a broad range of West African specialties in the $6.50 to $10.00 price range. These include *kenkey*, *banku*, *fufu*, *Joloff rice*, *toa*, and *gari*. Many of the dishes can be made with your choice of chicken, oxtail, beef, or fish, and a choice of sauces (or "soups," as the menu refers to them), which include peanut, *equishie* (sunflower seed), palm nut, and okra.

I had *fufu*, the national dish of Ghana, selecting the peanut option for sauce and the chicken option for meat. It arrived in a giant white bowl nearly 12 inches wide. Sitting in the thick peanut sauce was a loaf of *fufu*. *Fufu*, unlike, say, mashed potatoes, repels sauce so the ingredients do not mingle. As the chicken and peanut sauce are consumed, the *fufu*, rises up out of the sauce. The chicken is baked chicken, good but not remarkable. The peanut sauce is hot, but no particular spices are detectable. Bring a friend with you if you order this item–there is plenty for two. The menu also features lots of beans, plantains, and black eyed peas, as well as a vegetarian section.

KEUR N' DEYE

Brooklyn
737 Fulton St. bet. S. Elliot & S. Portland Sts.
(718) 875-4937
Subway stop: Lafayette Ave. on A or C train

The second restaurant my cabdriver mentioned restricts itself to "Senegalese Traditional Home Cooking," according to its business card. Senegalese cuisine is among the best in Africa, featuring fresh seafood and lots of vegetables including okra, yucca, yams, sweet potatoes, cabbage, calabaza, eggplant, and carrots.

The seafood and vegetables are essential elements of *tiebou dienn*, the national dish, affectionately referred to as *cheb*. How it's made: Chunks of fish, stuffed with green onion and parsley, are fried in palm oil. After the fish is cooked, it is removed and water is added to the oil remaining in the pot so an assortment of vegetables can be boiled. Then the vegetables are removed, and rice and a bit of tomato paste and hot pepper are added to the pan. When the rice–dyed a deep red by the palm oil–is done, it is heaped onto a serving platter with the vegetables and fish carefully arranged on top. If you cook *cheb* properly, a layer of rice remains "welded" to the bottom of the cooking pot. This delicacy is carefully scraped off and strewn across the top of the dish just before serving. The dish is eaten from a communal platter and the cook makes sure there is an equitable mixture of components for each diner.

The *cheb* here is nicely prepared, though presented nontraditionally in individual servings, with the rice, fish, and vegetables arranged separately on an attractive wooden plate–a bargain at $7.00. Other typical Senegalese dishes include chicken or beef *mafe* and fish *yassa*. Don't miss the homemade *bissap* (sorrel) and ginger drinks ($2.00 for a tall glass).

LUCKY STAR DELI
Manhattan
214 W. 50th St. bet. Broadway & 8th Ave.
(212) 571-6881
Subway stop: 49th St. on N or R train; 50th St. on 1 or 9 train

If you walk into the Lucky Star Deli about noon on a weekday, you'll see the kind of sandwich joint that is pandemic in Midtown. But come back a little after 2:00 P.M., bypass the sandwich queue and climb the stairs, and you'll find the scene is hopping with tall Senegalese men, many from the Joloff (pronounced "wool-off") tribe. Go through the swinging door marked *Not An Exit* and order your *cheb*. Four dollars gets you an enormous serving of rice, fresh tuna (!) stuffed with parsley, and six vegetables: carrots, yams, winter squash, cabbage, eggplant, and yucca. This *cheb*, is absolutely the original article, and you should hop on the subway and get some immediately. The African minions at the Lucky Star Deli concoct one home-style dish per day, alternating between *cheb*, *mafe*, and *yassa*. *Cheb* dominates the lineup.

NGONE INTERNATIONAL GOURMET
Manhattan
823 6th Ave. bet. 28th & 29th Sts.
(212) 967-7899
Subway stop: 34th St. on B, D, F, N, Q, or R train

First opened as a baloney-and-white-bread deli, Ngone International Gourmet eventually began to serve African food. Although disorganized the first time I tried it, the place turned out a very convincing *cheb* that included bluefish, cabbage, okra (disintegrated), carrots, yucca, and red pepper. On a subsequent visit, I sampled an excellent lamb *mafe*–many big chunks of lamb in a rich peanut sauce. (Ask for one of the bonnet peppers when you order this dish, and then watch out!) In recent months, the restaurant has evolved, and Senegalese food is now the main focus. It is one of the friendliest restaurants in town. As the menu says, "Chef Ousmane welcomes you!"

AFRICAN RESTAURANT
Bronx
1729 176th St. bet. Nelson St. & Macombs Rd.
(718) 901-0784
Subway stop: 176th St. on 4 train

Recommended by both a Peace Corps worker and another Ghanaian cabdriver, African Restaurant is located among the rolling hills of Morris Heights in the Bronx. But once you step inside the unprepossessing storefront, you might as well be in Accra. All food is served in carryout containers and eaten with the right hand; absolutely no utensils are available. The cuisine is strictly Ghanaian, consisting of mashes served with a variety of stews, called soups.

On a recent visit, a group of us enjoyed three mashes: *fufu*, made from fresh cassava root; *ebba*, made from *gari* (a meal of fermented cassava); and *emo-tuw*, kneaded glutinous rice. Each mash comes in a loaf form, which is wrapped in foil, then steamed.

Our waitress, resplendent in African headdress, brought us three soups. One, spinach-based and thickened with *egusi* (ground-up, toasted melon seed), contained a hunk of mutton and a chicken leg. The second, peanut-based with fresh ginger, garlic, and goat, was the spiciest and the best. The third, made with plenty of fresh okra, offered up mutton and little bits of red sweet pepper. The stews are eaten by grabbing a hunk of the mash with the right hand and dipping it in the stew. The preferred drink is water.

DEMU CAFE

Brooklyn
773 Fulton St. bet. S. Portland & S. Oxford Sts.
(718) 875-8484
Subway stop: Lafayette Ave. on A or C train

When you dine here, you are likely to be waited on by several different members of the Demu family during the course of your meal. Proprietor Ganiu M. Demu, wearing a Day-Glo green baseball cap, was our waiter. My companion and I shared a bowl of yam porridge, a dappled mixture of white and orange boiled yams, slightly mashed and flecked with plenty of crushed red pepper. The mild, meaty flavor tastes great. Also sampled: *amala*, a mash made from yam flour—moist, dark brown, and shaped like a small beret. Since mash is usually eaten with a soup, we asked for vegetable soup—a tomato and palm oil blend that was thick with a chopped, spinach-y green. We also ordered fish and goat, to be placed in the soup. Our fish portion–consisting of the front half of a bluefish and back half of a mackerel (at first it seemed like we'd stumbled on the results of a gene splicing experiment)–was good. But the three big chunks of goat were hard to get to, with fat, skin, and bones getting in the way of the meat.

The dining room is spacious and comfortable with nothing on the walls. A serving window looks into the kitchen, where the Demu daughters in pigtails can be seen playing. Each day the cafe has only a few of the dishes they list on the menu. Ask your Demu waiter what is available. If you want to eat with your right hand, the way most Africans do, the server will bring you a white plastic tub of water to wash with.

ASIAN MELTING POT

To most people, Asian cooking means Chinese, Indian, or Japanese. Maybe you've also tried Vietnamese, Korean, and Philippine. But what about all the other countries in this part of the world? In New York, you can sample Tibetan, Taiwanese, and Mongolian cooking, all influenced by the Chinese, but with many unique features as well. Here, for the aficionado, are restaurants that serve some of the more obscure Oriental cuisines available in New York. Behold the delicious variety and rejoice!

HENG HENG

Manhattan
43 Canal St. at intersection of Essex and E. Broadway
(212) 966-5419
Subway stop: E. Broadway on F train

Some of the newest, cheapest restaurants to hit Manhattan's ever-expanding Chinatown are

Malaysian. Heng Heng is one of the best. (Within a few blocks are three other Malaysian places, in case you want to experiment.) Malaysian food is a fascinating combination of Chinese, Indian, and Indonesian cooking styles, with something on the menu to please everyone. For devotees of bland food, there are delicious bowls of rice porridge, flavored with meat broth and green onions. My favorite, crispy pig intestine porridge ($2.75), contains several kinds of meat, none easily identifiable as pig intestines. The signature dish of Malaysian cuisine is fiery hot curry soup made with coconut milk and laced with red chili oil. It comes in several variations, with a meal-sized portion costing around $3.00 (and just try to finish it!).

KING'S CHINESE CUISINE AND MONGOLIAN BARBQ

Manhattan
153 W. 36th St. bet. 7th Ave. & Broadway
(212) 629-8602
Subway stop: 34th St. on 1, 2, 3, 9, B, D, F, or Q train

I'm a sucker for a restaurant with a gimmick. When I heard about a place with a big round griddle in the window, I ran right over. The front area of this spacious establishment is devoted to a gorgeous circular griddle, four feet in diameter, shiny new, and attended by two white-garbed "priests," all penned in by a Formica counter.

At one end of the counter are stacks of ample ceramic bowls. For $5.45 you fill one of these bowls as full as you can from the salad bar—style counter, starting with thin frozen curls of pork, chicken, and beef. Following the meat are trays of peppers, bean sprouts, Chinese cabbage, spinach, broccoli, cloud ear fungus, tomatoes, Spanish onions, green onions, celery, carrots, and noodles—all fresh and nicely presented. After heaping these ingredients into your bowl, proceed to the oil station where crocks labeled hot, garlic, ginger, diet, etc. stand filled with liquids resembling salad dressing. Stir vigorously before making your choice.

Now the ceremony: The chef/"priest" tugs the bowl from your hand and upends it onto the griddle. Wielding a metal spatula in his left hand, he vigorously pushes the ingredients across the griddle, containing the sliding ingredients with two outsize wooden chopsticks held in his right hand. The "priest" pays particular attention to the frozen meat chips, poking them repeatedly to make sure they cook. Aware of your astonishment, he makes a great display of his efforts. Finally proclaiming your food done, he dumps everything, including griddle scrapings, into a disposable aluminum container. Take it home or eat it there, your choice.

TIBET SHAMBALA

Manhattan
488 Amsterdam Ave. bet. W. 83rd & 84th Sts.
(212) 721-1270
Subway stop: 86th St. on 1, 9, B, or C train

In addition to the charming staff, Tibet Shambala offers food that is a culinary revelation and a peaceful atmosphere that makes patrons feel like whispering. Despite Chinese and Indian tinges, the palette of flavors is skewed in nearly unrecognizable directions. (One of the directions is bland, but this can be remedied with the excellent cilantro-based hot sauce.) The center of the cuisine is steamed or fried dumplings called *momo*; my favorite is the version filled with potatoes and cilantro called *shogo*–fried *momo* ($6.25). There are lots of vegetarian choices on the menu, including *thaba nenzom* ($7.25), a platter loaded with three cold salads featuring suprising ingredients including black-eyed peas, cauliflower, and tofu.

TAIPEI BIG RICE BOWLS

Queens
81-48 Baxter Ave. at 82nd St.
(718) 429-4818
Subway stop: Roosevelt Ave./Jackson Heights on E, F, G, or R train

Taiwanese food is *not* Chinese food. If you make the mistake of calling it Chinese food in this unpretentious restaurant, I won't be responsible for what they do. Nevertheless, Taiwanese includes many Chinese influences. Shanghai-style cold appetizers and entrées similar to Cantonese dishes are spiked with fresh basil and hot peppers. Traces of Japanese cuisine can be detected in the *maki*-type rolls in squid salad Taiwanese style ($6.65). Crisp, tasty omelets, like the panfried oyster cake ($3.95) jammed with freshly shucked oysters, have a Portuguese accent. Some of the most interesting items on the menu are uniquely Taiwanese, such as the meatball cake and Taiwanese rice cake ($1.65 each), which are both huge dumplings with a see-through covering made of sweet potato starch. Best choices for the first-time diner are clams with basil, panfried periwinkle, or transcendent eels with chives.

BARBECUE

STICK TO YOUR RIBS

Queens
5-16 51st Ave. off of Vernon Blvd.
(718) 937-3030
Subway stop: Vernon Blvd./Jackson Blvd. on 7 train

Proprietor Robert Pearson offers a large number of barbecued items, by the sandwich or by the pound. Choices include sliced beef brisket; chopped brisket; pork shoulder, sliced or chopped Carolina style with a vinegary tomato sauce; sausage; chicken; pork ribs; beef ribs (long or short); and lamb ribs. The chicken is crisp-skinned and moist on the inside. The beef ribs are charred at the tips; the meat, having spent eighteen hours in the pit, is falling off the bone.

Like all great barbecuers, Pearson has made some modest modifications in the formula. He has introduced great bread into a barbecue joint for the first time in history. Stick to Your Ribs makes sandwiches using crusty, torpe-do-shaped Portuguese rolls. After brushing sauce on both sides of a split roll, the counterperson drapes on a portion of barbecue (which he weighs on the scale, just to show how fair he is). The roll knocks the meat for a home run.

If weather permits, you can eat on the patio out back, where a huge red barbecue machine stands next to the rear wall of the building. Although tradition prompts us to call this a "pit," it is really an enclosed smoker, about eight feet high and seeping delicious smoke. There are three picnic tables with lattice metal tops so the barbecue sauce can drip through. Utterly without pretense, this joint would be worth finding even if you're a vegetarian and can't eat anything but the coleslaw and spoon pudding.

With Stick to Your Ribs in town, it's hard to imagine why anyone would want to eat barbecue anywhere else, but in case you do, here are several other places:

COWGIRL HALL OF FAME
Manhattan
519 Hudson St. at W. 10th St.
(212) 633-1133
Subway stop: Christopher St. on 1 or 9 train

The barbecue menu here is limited to brisket and beef ribs. The brisket, although copious, is a bit dry. But the ribs are great. You get five huge ones, plenty meaty, with sides of potato salad and coleslaw for $11.95. While this is not cheap, ribs rarely are. A couple more good things are the honey-dipped fried chicken and fried catfish. Portions are uniformly enormous.

EMILY'S
Manhattan
1325 5th Ave. at 111th St.
(212) 996-1212
Subway stop: 110th St. on 6 train

Emily's has a good combo of a quarter barbecued chicken and five pork ribs for $9.50. This is a soul food locale, and there is an extensive list of traditional sides–yams, black-eyed peas, collards, macaroni and cheese, rice and peas–from which you pick two. (Some of the sides–such as the collard greens, which are low in both fat and salt–have a health-food twist.) A hunk of corn bread also comes with your meal. The chopped barbecue, which is a dinner plateful of chopped pork with a sweet sauce, is a bargain at $7.95. Let it not go unmentioned that Emily's is a happening place to hang out.

VIRGIL'S REAL BARBECUE
Manhattan
152 W. 42nd St. bet. 6th & 7th Aves.
(212) 921-9494
Subway stop: Times Sq. on 1, 2, 3, 7, N, R, or S train

If any place deserves the name "barbecue emporium," Virgil's Real Barbecue does. This place tries to cover all the bases, serving several regional types of barbecue, as well as Southern cooking, grilled seafood, and even raw shellfish. Dinners run in the $10.95 to $24.95 range; the sandwich platters are more affordable. I sat at the lunch counter, which looks right into the kitchen, and ordered the $7.95 brisket sandwich. The platter arrived with plenty of meat on the sesame seed bun, a side of potato salad and "mustard slaw," and a half-sour pickle (weird in this context). The meat was moist and red-edged but slightly lacking in smoky flavor. (And I wished it had been sliced by hand, not by a slicing machine.) Five good sauces are provided on the table: three traditional slightly sweet tomato sauces in mild, medium, and hot; a North Carolina—style, vinegar-based sauce; and a Mexican hot sauce made in Jalisco.

On another visit I tried the Memphis pork ribs platter ($14.95), which included six meaty ribs, two sides of your choice, and jalapeño corn bread. The portions were so large I could have split the platter with someone else. Once again, though, they seem to have scrimped on the hardwood in the barbecuing process. Virgil's is not as good as Stick to Your Ribs, but depending on where you live, getting there may be a lot easier.

CHINESE

Thirty years ago, the Chinese food available in city eateries was likely to be Cantonese. Since then, relaxed relations with the People's Republic and the tremendous influx of capital from Hong Kong have allowed us to enjoy other forms of Chinese food in the expanding Chinatowns of Manhattan, Sunset Park in

Brooklyn, and Elmhurst and Flushing in Queens. Szechuan, Hunan, Hong Kong, Shanghai, Taiwanese, Chiu Chow, and a more sophisticated take on Cantonese food itself are widely available. If you've never tried the Chinese restaurants of the outer boroughs, you'll find their prices are usually cheaper and their atmosphere more homey than their Manhattan counterparts.

WONG KEE

Manhattan
113-117 Mott St. bet. Mott & Hester Sts.
(212) 226-9018 and (212) 966-1160
Subway stop: Canal St. on 6, J, N, or R train

It is an axiom that all eateries have at least one great

dish. In some Chinese restaurants, it's written in Chinese on a strip of pink paper hanging on the wall. At Wong Kee, the great dish is on the small "coffee shop" menu usually not offered to non-Chinese customers. You have to ask for the coffee shop menu when you sit down, and you'd better not ask for it after 6:00 P.M. The dish called Three Precious Ingredients over Rice ($4.65) makes an excellent late lunch or early supper. The three ingredients–sweet anise-baked pork, sliced steamed chicken, and a cold fried egg–are artfully arranged on a heaping plate of rice with brown sauce that is poured over most Chinese barbecue. On the very top is a salty green sauce thick with green onions and fresh ginger. Do not accept the dish if the green sauce is not present. Send it back and have it added. The green sauce makes even the cold fried egg taste great. The combination of flavors is devastating.

SUN GOLDEN ISLAND RESTAURANT
Manhattan
1 Elizabeth St. at Bayard St.
(212) 274-8787
Subway stop: Canal St. on 6, J, N, or R train

Until a few years ago, this restaurant was one of the only places in New York where you could find Chiu Chow cooking, a subtly spiced variation on Cantonese concocted by Chinese expatriates living in

Southeast Asia with an emphasis on seafood and noodle dishes. Skip the appetizers and go right to the entrées. Crab is the best deal of all. Crab with chin-gens sauce ($8.95) is a good-sized plate of four hacked-up Dungeness crabs (enough for two people) with a briny sauce of ginger and black beans. Try the house specialty, fried e-fu noodles Chiu-Chow style ($7.95)–a nest of thin, deep-fried noodles with white sugar and wine vinegar poured on top.

HONG KONG SEAFOOD
Queens
40-48 Main St. near 44th Ave.
(718) 961-3302
Subway stop: Main St./Flushing on 7 train

You can spend a little or a lot here. Chinese barbecue over rice is available at low prices, as are soups, dim sum, and bakery products. The dim sum appetizer for two ($5.50) offers four pieces each of steamed shrimp dumplings and pleasantly crunchy steamed wontons with pork and water chestnuts. All of the Chinese families dining around us were enjoying a bean curd appetizer, which consisted of a huge mound of fried bean curd squares, with several sauces on the side. (The Hong Kong sauces are unexpected: One tastes like anchovies and red wine vinegar, another is mustard based, the third is a fiery red chili paste.) After the appetizers, we splurged on some of the menu's higher priced entrées. The best was squid with sour vegetables ($7.75) in a semisweet brown sauce with red and green bell peppers and hunks of pickled cabbage. (Anything here with pickled cabbage in it is good.) Even more tender (in fact, overtenderized) was the stir-fried conch ($13.95), silky slices of conch in a salty garlic sauce. With its broad range of dishes and prices, Hong Kong Seafood solves the problem of choosing among the twenty or so other Chinese restaurants cramming the area.

DUMPLINGS AND THINGS

SUN HOP SHING TEA HOUSE

Manhattan
21 Mott St. bet. Chatham Sq. & Moscow St.
(212) 267-2729
Subway stop: Canal St. on 6, J, N, or R train

Most people prefer to eat dim sum, the teahouse cuisine of China, at restaurants where the dining rooms are as big as football fields and where total strangers are seated cheek-by-jowl at huge tables like in the school lunchroom. As the carts go around the room, the plates of dumplings become progressively colder and more dried out. I prefer this tiny place with ten tables, where the distance from the kitchen to the front door is only about thirty feet. After each cart passes with its single variety, the plates that are not purchased are stacked in a glass-fronted steam case at the front of the restaurant. This allows the dim sum to stay fresh, and lets you order any one you want at your convenience, without waiting for the appropriate cart to appear.

Still, it's best when it comes right from the kitchen. An excellent plate here is fried taro–lacy cakes made like latkes out of shredded taro root–starchy with a nutty sweetness and crunchy exterior. Another eye-opener is the stuffed bean curd, half a pillow of firm curd, cut on the diagonal and stuffed with a mixture of pork, ginger, and green onion. And don't miss the bean curd skin roll–pork filling in a thin, rubbery wrapper–one of the most successful bean curd delivery systems ever invented!

Avoid the mushy shrimp balls, bland wontons, and the beef ball. Nearly everything else is great.

EXCELLENT DUMPLING HOUSE

Manhattan
111 Lafayette St. just south of Canal St.
(212) 219-2333
Subway stop: Canal St. on 6, J, N, or R train

This small restaurant, which prides itself on its dumplings, has much in its favor, especially at the cheaper end of its menu. Fresh-tasting scallion pancakes are lighter and much less greasy than the usual sodden version. At $1.50 an order, they're a bargain. Culinary wonders called rice cakes turn out to be blocks of noodlelike material, wok-fried with garlic, green onions, and other fried rice—type ingredients. The Shanghai Fried Rice (about $5.00) happily unites many of the fish and meat ingredients normally found in carryout Chinese food. Another outstanding dish is the forbidding-sounding Sliced Fish and Sour Cabbage: fresh hunks of cod (or similar) fish that are battered, deep-fried, and then wok-fried with tangy strands of pickled sweet-and-sour cabbage and other greens. Avoid the "sizzling" dishes on the menu. Not only higher priced, they're usually cloaked in the sweet, French dressing—like sauce, often found on Szechuan baby shrimp dishes.

BEEF JERKY

Manhattan
68 E. Broadway at Market St.
(212) 226-6858
Subway stop: E. Broadway on F train

At the corner of East Broadway and Market Street, a couple of doors toward Confucius Plaza, is a very narrow storefront that sells Chinese barbecue. Behind the grill, with its stainless steel grate at the front of the store, is a counter where flat squares of raw beef and pork are lined up waiting to be cooked. Further down the counter, a box with a warming bulb holds the finished product for sale at $7.20 a pound. The beef is striated and chewy, like jerky, and has been glazed with a sugar and anise sauce prior to barbecuing. The pork is much spicier and constructed from compressed pork fragments. Since there are no bones, skin, or (visible) fat, one pound is enough for four moderately hungry people.

MEE NOODLE SHOP & GRILL

Manhattan
219 1st Ave. at E. 13th St.
(212) 995-0333
Subway stop: 1st Ave. on L train

Manhattan
922 2nd Ave. at E. 49th St.
(212) 888-0318
Subway stop: 50th St. on 6 train

Until recently, the original Mee on 13th Street and 1st Avenue was unique north of Chinatown for its authentic noodle soup and meat-hanging-in-the-window cuisine. (Now this type of place seems to be found on every block in Manhattan.) In this Chinese coffee shop a short list of ingredients can be combined in endless assortments as soups and over rice. Let me quote from the menu:

We Have 6 Kinds of Noodle, Please Specify

1. Spinach Noodle (Linguine)

2. Mandarin Noodle (Linguine)
3. Lo Mein (Spaghetti)
4. Thin Cantonese Noodle (Angel Hair)
5. Mee Fun (Thin Rice Noodle)
6. Chow Fun (Flat Soft Rice Noodle)

CHINESE

These six kinds of noodles can be matched with ten different toppings, including shrimp, duck, roast pork, and soy sauce chicken. But wait! Next the menu reveals the rules of combining:

Remember:
a. To name the noodle of your choice
b. No charge to change noodle to cantonese wonton
c. To add cantonese wonton pay $1.00 extra
d. To add meat, pay $1.50 per meat
e. To add hard boiled egg pay $.50 each

Dining here is an intellectual exercise. At first I sat wondering how many combinations of the six noodles, ten toppings, and additional options were possible. (I assumed that you could have more than one ingredient from the second and third lists.) Perhaps, I thought, the answer could be arrived at by some formula like (10 X 6 X 2) + (9 X 5 X 1) + (8 X 4) + (7 X 3) + (6 X 2) + (5 X 1) + (4 X 1) + (3 X 1) + (2 X 1) + (1 X 1), which equals 245 possibilities. I now realize that this answer is not correct.

The other Mee location is virtually identical.

ZEN PALATE

Manhattan
34 Union Sq. E. at E. 16th St.
(212) 614-9345
Subway stop: Union Sq. on 4, 5, 6, L, N, or R train

Manhattan
663 9th Ave. at W. 46th St.
(212) 582-1669
Subway stop: 50th St. on C or E train

With its green anodized copper exterior fronting Union Square, Zen Palate is the hippest Chinese restaurant in town. Skip the expensive restaurant upstairs and head for the reasonably priced Zen Palate Gourmet Shop. The food on both levels is strictly vegetarian, from the school of Chinese cuisine that attempts to fabricate vegetarian look-alikes for meat, fish, and fowl.

The downstairs menu includes twenty-three appetizers designated "Tasty Morsels." Scallion pancakes ($3.50) are good-sized and slightly less greasy than usual. An exceedingly odd but welcome twist is the pancakes "sandwich," a thin slice of TVP (textured vegetable protein) that has the color and flavor of ham; the whole affair is glued together with plum sauce. Other interesting-sounding morsels include topi brown rice maki with a side salad, fajita home-style, and stir-fried spinach linguine with vegetables.

The heart of the menu is a list of twenty main dishes that are served with a scoop of brown rice and two small egg rolls. The dishes include an eggplant in garlic sauce ($6.50) made remarkable by the bed of stir-fried hearts of bok choy upon which the eggplant rests.

The Zen Palate concept is more interesting than its execution. Eating vegetarian is good for the planet, but any health benefits you might enjoy are outdistanced by the saltiness and greasiness of the food. (The original West Side Zen Palate is a less impressive architectural achievement, but it's a good place to get a vegetarian meal in the theater district.)

CUBAN

The first period of Cubans–mainly intellectuals–emigrating to New York began in the mid-1800s and ended with Cuban independence in 1898. The next wave occurred during the dictatorship of Batista in the 1950s. The most recent was in the early 1960s, with those fleeing Fidel Castro. During this last period a unique subgroup of Cubans, the Cuban Chinese, arrived. Brought to Cuba before the First World War to work in the sugarcane fields, they had become Cuban over the years in every regard but race: They spoke Spanish, dressed in guayaberas, and mastered the art of Cuban cooking. Here are several restaurant standbys and a Cuban-Chinese newcomer.

SAM CHINITA

Manhattan
176 8th Ave. bet. W. 18th & 19th Sts.
(212) 741-0240
Subway stop: 14th St. on A, C, or E train

Plenty of the 5,000 Cuban Chinese who came to New York in the 1960s opened restaurants, especially on

Chelsea's 8th Avenue, the Upper West Side of Manhattan, and along the Grand Concourse in The Bronx. The best in Chelsea is Sam Chinita, which occupies an old diner on 8th Avenue—one of those squat structures with a shiny metal exterior made to look like a railroad dining car. The architecture happily meshes with the antique quality of the food. As at any Cuban-Chinese restaurant, ignore the Chinese side of the menu, which contains bland Cantonese dishes, imperfectly remembered from the 20s, and go straight to the Cuban side, where you'll find the food that the Cuban Chinese themselves prefer to eat. These dishes are prepared with gusto, and can be judged on an equal footing with the slightly different versions found in regular Cuban restaurants.

CHRYSANTHEMUM

Manhattan
199 8th Ave. bet. W. 20th & 21st Sts.
(212) 989-1116
Subway stop: 23rd St. on C or E train

An exception to the "Cuban side only" rule is Chrysanthemum, a newly opened Cuban-Chinese joint on 8th Avenue, across the street and a little bit up from Sam Chinita. The Chinese part of the menu has been updated to augment the old-hat Cantonese dishes with Szechuan entrées and even some health-conscious Chinese fare. The result isn't half bad, and is particularly useful if you and a group of friends cannot agree on where to dine. On a recent visit, chicken fried rice ($2.75) easily satisfied two eight year-old diners, while their beleagured parents dined Cuban style. Unfortunately, the Cuban cooking here is slightly below par. The signature dish of Havana cuisine, *pernil asado* (garlicky pork roast), was made with pork filets, rather than carved off a giant hunk of pig, and it lacked the oily herb-flecked patina and jagged, flavorful pieces (including skin) that you should expect.

HAVANA CHELSEA LUNCHEONETTE
Manhattan
190 8th Ave. bet. W. 19th. & 20th Sts.
(212) 243-9421
Subway stop: 23rd St. on C or E train

This amazing Cuban greasy spoon has a refrigerator case with a window on the street, so you can look in at all the good stuff: individual servings of flan and coconut pudding, big ceramic bowls of octopus salad and salt cod salad, and slices of pork waiting to be incorporated into the best-selling Cuban sandwich. Made on Italian loaves with layers of roast pork, boiled ham, Swiss cheese, and pickles, the sandwiches are placed into a two-surface press (called a Cuban sandwich maker) that toasts, melts, smashes, crisps, and generally anneals the sandwich–to the benefit of the bread and the fillings. Cuban sandwiches come in two sizes–*mediano* ($3.25) and *grande* ($3.75), which could be called "humongo." *Pulpo* salad ($4.75), made with rubbery chunks of boiled octopus, onion, green pepper, celery, and pimiento–all marinated in oil and vinegar–is also highly recommended. *Yucca* ($3.00) is another estimable offering. The starchy root vegetable is boiled to a consistency more yielding than usual (that's good). Make sure you get the garlic sauce that makes this dish great.

NATIONAL CAFE
Manhattan
210 1st Ave. bet. E. 12th & 13th Sts.
(212) 473-9354
Subway stop: 1st Ave. on L train

The corner of 13th Street and 1st Avenue is the epicenter of East Village good eats. Across the street from Mee (page 24) is the original Christine's, where you'll find good challah French toast and soups. Even better is the National Cafe, a Cuban joint run by a family of women who make excellent pork roast, fricassee chicken, black beans, and yellow rice. It's one of the best places to eat in the East Village, but don't everybody go at once. There are only three tables and a few counter stools. Carryout, however, is always an option.

EURASIAN CATCHALL

For cuisines that are relatively familiar to New Yorkers, such as Greek and German, this chapter includes a couple of token restaurants that are way above average and worthy of representation in this survey of good and cheap ethnic eats. The Uzbekistan is, as far as I know, the sole city avatar of its national cuisine. Here's a category of lonely, miscellaneous restaurants.

ELIAS CORNER

Queens
24-01 31st St. bet. 24th Ave. & 24th Rd.
(718) 932-1510
Subway stop: Astoria Blvd. on N train

Unlike the diners that barely nod to Greek cuisine, but whose decor hits you over the head with Parthenons and Greek-key patterns, the decor at Elias Corner is resolutely non-Hellenic. With its display of various seagoing knots and an oil painting of Moby Dick (or some other whale), it could easily be mistaken for a seafood restaurant, which it is.

The restaurant takes fresh whole fish and either throws it onto a charcoal grill until it is black or lightly flours and deep-fries it. Having been raised to avoid fried foods, I insisted our party opt for the grill. This proved highly successful with the red snapper. We paid $12.00 for a tender, delicious fish that served two. The St. Peter's fish weathered the grill treatment less well, owing to its smaller size (a higher percentage of char to flesh) and its subtler flavor. The swordfish kebabs were overdone but I enjoyed the pepper, onion, and tomato chunks served with them. As we were leaving the restaurant, I saw a plate of beautifully fried red mullet and deeply regretted not ordering them. With four of us eating the fresh whole fish on a par with Manhattan's finest seafood restaurants, along with some stellar side dishes and a bottle of decent Greek wine, the total came to $84.00. (E.M.)

UNCLE GEORGE'S GREEK TAVERN
Queens
34-19 Broadway at 34th St.
(718) 626-0593
Subway stop: Broadway on N train

Uncle George's, on the other hand, looks like a Greek diner, which it is. Revolving in the window on a brace

EURASIAN CATCHALL

33

of spits are a pig and a lamb, while at another rotis-serie inside the restaurant, a chorus line of 100 or so chickens turn. The waiters are expert at ignoring you. Every once in a while, one of them goes running down the central aisle carrying an eight-foot sword rammed through a pig on the way to the rotisserie.

The large entrées range from $7.00 to $10.00 and include several lemony-salty, roasted potato halves. Roast pork consists of a full pound of meat, cut in inch-and-a-half cubes, some fatty and some lean, rubbed with sage, salt, and pepper before roasting, and sprinkled with dried oregano. (Dried oregano is sprinkled on top of nearly everything here.) Thick rings of battered and deep fried squid are pretty good, but come with only a couple of lemon wedges and no dipping sauce.

A good starter is *tzatziki*–a plate of yogurt mixed with cucumber, chopped onion, and loads of raw garlic. You spread it on bread (an excellent crusty, torpedo-shaped loaf). A pleasant version of the egg-plant dish called *imam* consists of whole eggplants overstewed with tomato, onion, and lots of oil. This special is available on Saturdays, also the only day you can savor rabbit and onion stew. The restaurant's best deal is the tiny aluminum carafe of *retsina*, the Greek wine flavored with resin from the casks in which it is stored, for $1.00.

SILVER SWAN

Manhattan
41 E. 20th St. bet. Broadway & Park Ave. So.
(212) 254-3611
Subway stop: 23rd St. on 6, N, or R train

Since the demise of the Ideal Restaurant in Manhattan's Yorkville (the last holdout from the days when East 86th Street was lined with German businesses and English was spoken with a thick German accent), I get my cheap German food in this new restaurant. The place looks very German inside, with comfortable booths, beer signs, and an imposing bar in the front room. To enjoy the bar menu, which has several unadorned German favorites at prices discounted from the dining room (where boar is king), you must sit in the front room or at the bar. You can, for example, get a good-sized portion of two *weisswurst*, bratwurst, or knockwurst, hot potato salad, and red cabbage or sauerkraut for $8.95. Goulash and sauerbraten are also available. A full list of German beers, including seven wheat beers served in half-liter flasks, is another magnet to draw you to this place.

HAPPY END

Brooklyn
924 Manhattan Ave. at Kent St.
(718) 383-9862
Subway stop: Greenpoint Ave. on G train

The cuisine here will be instantly familiar to anyone familiar with the Polish coffee shops that dot the East Village. The menu board reads in Polish with a chalkboard offering the dishes in English as an afterthought.

On my first visit, a group of us sat for ten minutes before realizing that there is no wait service and that we would have to queue up in front of the register to order. A woman of amazing girth is seen through the door of the tiny kitchen, swinging pots in every direction, assembling the dinners with deadly accuracy. A hunk of meat is deftly scooped from a deep container on the steam table, then slung on a plate with mashed potatoes and paprika gravy. Next, identical mounds of two barely distinguishable salads are heaped on: Cabbage salad and carrot-and-cabbage salad. The same presentation on every plate makes this one of the most single-minded dining places in the world—and one of the cheapest. All dinners are $4.00 or $5.00. And like it says on the menu, a free beverage is provided; undersweetened orange Kool-Aid that you serve yourself from a plastic beverage dispenser on a card table.

UZBEKISTAN KEBAB HOUSE

Manhattan
789 9th Ave. bet. W. 52nd & 53rd Sts.
(212) 664-0123
Subway stop: 50th St. on C or E train

A former state in the south central region of the former Soviet Union, Uzbekistan is now an independent country. Uzbekistan Kebab House is a thumbnail-sized eatery on a strip of upper 9th Avenue jammed with ethnic restaurants. It's hard to imagine a smaller dining room or kitchen. Most of the cooking gets done in the hearth, which has a glowing charcoal fire covered by a grate.

The dining room is decorated with colorful Persian miniatures and framed photos of Islamic architecture and archaeological excavation sites. Lamb kebab ($7.00) comes off the skewer–ten pieces of lamb that were a little tough but flavorful. It rests on a generous bed of fragrant pilaf made with basmati rice, yellow raisins, and carrots. Also on the plate is a salad of iceberg lettuce and cucumbers, dressed with extra thick yogurt flecked with dried oregano. Another entrée, described on the menu as "Half Chicken," is barbecued with a yogurt and spice coating. You'd swear you were eating tandoori chicken with the skin left on. Side orders of vegetables, including spinach, zucchini, okra, eggplant and "cauliflowers," are available ($2.00 each). The only dessert on the menu is a rice pudding that comes in an elegant glass dish. It's silky smooth, with no visible grains of rice, flavored with cardamom, and topped with crushed pistachios.

AFGHAN KEBAB HOUSE

Manhattan
764 9th Ave. bet. W. 51st & 52nd Sts.
(212) 307-1612
Subway stop: 50th St. on C or E train

As in most Afghan restaurants, each table here is covered with a small Persian rug, then with a sheet of glass. Unlike most Afghan restaurants, however, this one displays a huge hammered copper bas-relief of Afghanistan on the wall. A recent meal commenced with *aushak*—Afghan dumplings, halfway between *pansoti* and *kreplach*—that are filled with scallions, then covered with homemade yogurt. My companion and I shared a lamb *kofta* kebab (finely minced lamb molded around a skewer and then grilled) and a fish kebab that featured very nice chunks of cod. Each plate came with flavorful rice, an iceberg lettuce—based salad with homemade yogurt, and a quite delicious piece of flat ridged Afghan bread sprinkled with black sesame seeds. (E.M.)

HAITIAN

Flatbush Avenue going north from Brooklyn College (near Nostrand Avenue) is a Little Port-Au-Prince, with Haitian travel agencies, car services, groceries, restaurants, even a storefront radio station. Explore this area and the other not-too-distant Haitian district centered at Rutland Road and Rockaway Parkway, and you'll find a good number of small, pleasant eateries where little English is spoken and the food is a tasty combination of African and French. One of the best is:

EVE'S RESTAURANT
Brooklyn
1366 Flatbush Ave. bet. E. 26th St. & Farragut Rd.
(718) 859-4874
Subway stop: Flatbush Ave./Brooklyn College on 2 or 5 train

It's a pleasant room, simple and spotless—eight tables with red and white tablecloths, ceramic seashells filled with paper napkins, and red artificial flowers. A woman in a white apron is seen cooking through a door at the rear of the room. Even though it was 12:30 P.M., lunch was not yet being served. So

I had breakfast, a choice of cornmeal or plantains served with fish, beef liver, or cow's feet. I picked the cornmeal and was served a plate loaded with cornmeal and pink beans cooked in fish stock—a very African-style mash. Accompanying the cornmeal was a small bowl of stewed cow's feet, big squares of foot flesh with a gelatinous, rubbery texture (maybe not for everyone), in a delicious broth, seasoned with thyme, garlic, carrots, and onion. I poured the stew over the cornmeal and dug in.

For those who prefer to dine in Manhattan, one of the last remaining vestiges of what was a thriving Haitian community in the 1960s and 70s is:

LE SOLEIL
Manhattan
877 10th Ave. bet. W. 57th & 58th Sts.
(212) 581-6059
Subway stop: 59th St./Columbus Cir. on A, B, C, D, 1, or 9 train

Favored by Haitian cabdrivers, this restaurant boasts a dining room decorated with brightly colored paintings of palm trees and island huts and innumerable pictures of Jean-Bertrand Aristide. The all-male clientele converses amiably and eats with evident gusto. There is a different menu for each day of the week of eight or so dishes (all $8.00 to $9.00). When I stopped by, three were available. I ordered the conch (*lambi*) and a fried red fish with sauce. The *lambi* was smothered in brown sauce tasting of garlic and onions, with the small pieces of conch having the texture and taste of fishy pork. The fish–a red snapper strewn with onions and sweet red peppers in a spicy red sauce laced with vinegar–was large and done to perfection. All entrées are accompanied by plain rice cooked with beans or white rice with soupy red beans on the side. You also get a whole boiled plantain. The servings are so large they have be to put in two containers if you're carrying out; one serving could easily be shared by two at lunch.

INDIAN

The stretch of Lexington Avenue between 27th and 34th Streets is host to a slew of inexpensive Indian restaurants. Several of my favorites there and elsewhere are:

EAST IN THE WEST

Manhattan
113 Lexington Ave. bet. E. 27th & 28th Sts.
(212) 683-1313
Subway stop: 28th St. on 6 train

The north side of the awning says "Indian delicacy created here;" the south side, "Pamper your taste the Indian way." For $4.75, the vegetarian special includes three choices from the six main dishes. I had *mattar paneer* (peas and fresh cheese). The little burnished boxcars of cheese were tender and fresh. Dal (a sauce/soup/stew made from lentils and split peas) was my second choice, made spicy and thick with large yellow split peas. Third was a vegetable stew containing potatoes, eggplant, tomatoes, green pepper, and summer squash—bland, but good with the others. The glory of the restaurant is the nan (here called tandoori roti) that comes with your meal, a brown and glistening bread, attractively flopped across a wicker basket and over a square foot in size. Take plenty of condiments from the Formica sideboard. The cilantro chutney is chunky and homemade. The cucumber-yogurt *raita* is thick. Toasted fennel seeds are a welcome addition to the usual selection.

CURRY IN A HURRY

Manhattan
119 Lexington Ave. bet. E. 27th & 28th Sts.
(212) 683-0904
Subway stop: 28th St. on 6 train

In this new location, the first Indian fast food restaurant on the "Little India" stretch of Lexington is as spacious as before. In the window facing Lexington Avenue, two tandoori pits stand on a ceramic tile counter along with a grill for making South Indian vegetarian specialties formerly available only on weekends. The unique chutney bar supplements the usual fast-food condiments—green chiles, raw onion, yogurt, cilantro and coconut chutney, tamarind chutney, salad stuff, lemon wedges—with new choices, including an astringent pickle of green olives, chile pepper, and lime pickle.

Guys who were hash slingers in the old locale have become demanding, suit-wearing supervisors in the new, and the quality and variety of the food have been ratcheted up a notch or two. The vegetarian special, consisting of two steam table dishes, with rice, nan, salad, and selections from the chutney bar, is $5.49. The same combo plus one meat dish is $5.99. The chicken I chose–pieces of boneless tandoori chicken breast in a creamy tomato sauce–was subtly flavored with garlic, cumin, and all the usual spices. *Mattar paneer* was too mild and slightly deficient in cheese. The cauliflower and potato curry and another made with mixed vegetables were well-prepared and flavorful.

MADRAS MAHAL

Manhattan
104 Lexington Ave. bet. E. 27th & 28th Sts.
(212) 684-4010
Subway stop: 28th St. on 6 train

A tremendous find for both vegetarians and Orthodox Jews, this kosher Indian restaurant serves vegetarian specialties from three cuisines: South Indian, Mogul, and Gujarati. The crisp, luxuriantly sized crepes filled with potatoes called *masala dosai* (about $6.00) are the best in town. The Gujarati menu, a restaurant rarity, includes a dal-based stew of eggplant, black-eyed peas, yams, and snow peas (*undhiyu*), as well as a couple of don't-miss appetizers: *kachori*, deep-fried fritters made with sweet peas and chickpeas that are a brilliant green when you bite into them, and *bhel puri*, a sweet-and-sour salad made with puffed rice. Service can be slow so go when you can enjoy a relaxed meal.

JACKSON DINER

Queens
37-0374 74th St. bet. 37th St. & Roosevelt Ave.
(718) 672-1232
Subway stop: Roosevelt Ave./Jackson Heights on
E, F, G, R, or 7 train

Near the end of the block lined with Indian business-es selling saris, jewelry, and electronic goods is the Jackson Diner. Inside, it *looks* just like a diner–one that serves Indian food. From the extensive list of appetizers, we tried the *pakora* ($1.75), eight surpris-ingly light vegetable fritters containing either cauli-flower, potato, or onion, or some combination of these three. The steamed lentil flour dumplings, called *iddly* had the right grassy edge, and were served with a slightly sour red lentil gruel (*sambar*) that was made chunky with tomato, potato, onions, and hot green peppers.

Main dishes ($7.00 to $9.00) were uniformly good. One of the more interesting non-vegetarian specials is *murg kadai*, small pieces of chicken tossed with fresh herbs and cooked in an earthenware Indian pan called a *kadai*. Highly recommended chicken *korma*, chicken tidbits in a mild yogurt and cashew

45

sauce, is available as a luncheon special. Available Monday through Friday only, from 11:30 A.M. to 4:00 P.M., these specials are a couple of dollars less than prices at other times.

Among the vegetarian specials, *baingan bhurta*–broiled eggplant cooked with onions, tomatoes, chiles, and fresh ginger, which gives the dish a sweet edge–is particularly good. Also commendable are the dishes featuring *paneer*, fresh curd cheese that has been pressed and briefly sautéed. The dal, made of dark brown lentils flavored with clove and cinnamon and served on the side without charge, is a revelation here. The waiters, thoughtful without being annoyingly obsequious, deserve special mention. They even leave a pitcher of ice water on the table so you can drink as much as you want.

DIMPLE INDIAN FAST FOOD

Queens
72-31 37th Ave. at 73rd St.
(718) 458-8144
Subway stop: Roosevelt Ave./Jackson Heights on E, F, G, R, or 7 train

Signs in the window of this new informal vegetarian eatery declare "We Serve Fresh Sugar Cane Juice" and "Big-Bite Frankie–$1.75." Inside, the smart black tile walls are set off by the four red tabletops. Most of the dishes are $2.50, and each plate contains two or more components. You can put together a meal of two or three plates or dine lightly on one. A typical selection, puri shak, includes two puris–not freshly made and a bit greasy–with chutney and your choice of steam table selections. One day the steam table options included vegetable *kofta*, okra and potatoes, dry eggplant curry, and *chana masala*, chickpeas with red sauce. Deep-fried potato patties in various shapes figure prominently here. Ragda patties, two deep-fried potato pancakes submerged in a chickpea soup, are sprinkled with raw onions. The "big-bite frankie," a potato patty formed into the shape of a hot dog, is served in a conventional hot dog bun with slices of cucumber and onion and a sweet-hot red pepper chutney. A variation called the "big bite" features the same ingredients wrapped in a pliable whole wheat flat bread called roti. Whether you choose the frankie or the big bite, ask for it to be warmed in the microwave.

JAMAICAN

Of all the Caribbean Islands, Jamaica has the most interesting and varied cuisine. It makes abundant use of fresh seafood, chicken, and pork and uses a broad range of flavors from an exciting variety of sources. Chinese indentured workers introduced soy sauce. African slaves provided green onions, cilantro, many of the cooking techniques, and the love of garlic and hot peppers. The Spanish, both directly and via Spanish-speaking Caribbean islands, introduced the use of salt cod and cooking techniques involving yellow onions, green peppers, and vinegar. Curries came directly from India and via England and Trinidad.

Jamaicans also cook with unusual botanicals: akee, which resembles scrambled eggs when cooked, breadfruit, and allspice, an indigenous spice resembling outsized peppercorns that Jamaican cooking–especially the technique known as jerking–makes spectacular use of.

In Jamaica, jerking is usually done in a busy open-air market or by the side of the road, using a sixty-gallon drum, split and hinged so it functions as a barbecue grill and a smoker. Recipes vary, but the jerk coating in which the meat is barbecued usually contains green onions, ground all-spice, garlic, fiery Scotch bonnet peppers, and soy sauce. The distinctive flavor of this dish derives in equal part from the cooking technique and the odd combination of flavorings. Jerked chicken (and pork) are available everywhere in Jamaica, and once you've tried them, you'll never forget the flavor.

SUGAR REEF

Manhattan
93 2nd Ave. bet. E. 5th & 6th Sts.
(212) 477-8427
Subway stop: Astor Pl. on 6 train

This is the only place in Manhattan that serves good jerk chicken. Here the chicken is actually charcoal grilled, the coating is thick and gritty with allspice, and the flavor is piquant. It's the best dish on the menu by far.

HARRY'S JERK CENTER

Bronx
1296 E. Gun Hill Rd. at Burke Ave.
(718) 798-4966
Subway stop: Gun Hill Rd. on 5 train

To get really authentic jerk, head for a jutting promontory at the confluence of Burke Avenue and East

Gunhill Road in the Williamsbridge section of the Bronx. The six small tables and smaller kitchen of Harry's Jerk Center can be seen through a thick plastic window, which displays three bottles of Aunt Linda's Colonic Bitters. Inside and outside, you can smell the quintessential ingredient of great jerk: smoke.

Whether you order a big jerk dinner for $7.50 or a small one for $5.50, your meal comes in an aluminum carryout container. The fragrant jerk lies on top of Jamaican rice and peas–pink beans and white rice stewed with sweet coconut milk–with a homemade hot pepper vinegar poured over everything. You can have the sauce hot or medium, or omit it entirely. Other specialties include: oxtails, brown smothered chicken, curry chicken, curry goat, fried or steamed fish (takes 30 minutes), and akee. Soups include pepper pot, cow cod, fish tea, and mannish water.

ROTI STAND

Manhattan
Open-air market at E. 125th St. & Lenox Ave.
Subway stop: 125th St. on 2 or 3 train

At the corner of 125th Street and Lenox Avenue, now known as Malcolm X Boulevard, is an open-air market. The most conspicuous commodity for sale is African handicrafts, but at the northern edge of the market is a roti stand with an awning shielding it from the sun. Roti is a pliable, whole wheat flat bread that originated in India, was brought to Trinidad by Indian immigrants, and then washed ashore in nearby Jamaica where it is especially prized by the Rastafarians. Roti is either filled with a relatively dry filling (so you can pick it up) or smothered in a wet one. Either way, it's a great lunch. The rotis are kept folded up in an electrically heated dutch oven, and you can have yours with vegetable, goat, chicken, or beef filling. For my goat roti, the vendor carefully unfolded the bread onto the table, dropped two large spoonfuls of thick potato and chickpea stew in the middle, then dumped two spoonfuls of mildly curried goat on top of the vegetables. She gave it a couple of shots of a hot sauce that looked homemade, and then folded up the package and placed it inside a couple of thicknesses of wax paper. For $4.00 it makes a very filling lunch. Just watch out for the bones in the goat.

JAVA HOUSE

Manhattan
162 Ave. B bet. E. 10th & 11th Sts.
Subway stop: 1st Ave. on L train

Seating is extremely limited: two red bar stools at the L-shaped black Formica counter plus two chairs at a table pushed against the wall. All the action is behind the counter, where the chef shuttles between the gleaming stove and big new steam table. He pauses to check a furiously boiling cauldron of *ital*, the vegetarian cuisine favored by Rastafarians. If the *ital* is ready, order it. If not, order the chicken roti ($5.00), drenched with curry gravy and dotted with whole peppercorns, allspice berries, and fresh thyme, or try the jerked chicken. It's not grilled over charcoal, alas, but nevertheless the skin remains crisp and intact in its piquant stewing sauce.

ROYAL BAKE SHOP
Bronx
215A E. 170th St. bet. Grand Concourse & Sheraton Ave.
(718) 681-9160
Subway stop: 170th St. on 4, C, or D train

What a contrast between the beef patties they sell at pizza parlors and the ones served here! The pastry, yellow with annato-colored shortening, is fresh and light. The filling is very spicy, with the meat ground so fine it's almost pureed. Patties are $1.00 each; two would make a fine, filling lunch. Eat them as the Jamaicans do, in a *coco* bread (70¢). As specialized as a hot dog bun, this yeast bread has been folded prior to baking to make a shape like a baseball glove. By itself the *coco* bread would be dull, but the combination of bread and patty is sublime–the spicy filling of the patty shining through two carbo layers, one puffy, one oily. Royal Bake Shop doesn't seem to sell much else, but these are good enough to warrant a special visit.

LA MADAMA CAFE & BAKERY

Manhattan
170 9th Ave. bet. W. 20th & 21st Sts.
(212) 255-0779
Subway stop: 23rd St. on E train

The magenta walls have gold accents. The pink granite-topped tables are set with antique flatware and deep blue paisley-edged plates. This thimble-sized Jamaican joint in Chelsea is pleasantly overdecorated with rococo framed shelves displaying jars of sauces and condiments (for sale), and voodoo statuettes, including the eponymous La Madama, a smiling, capaciously figured woman with bandanna-wrapped hair. What's best here is the delicious salt cod fritters, dense with fish and green onion and flecked with fresh red chiles and black pepper. There is a limited luncheon menu with a single different main dish each day. These include calypso chicken, shrimp gumbo, oxtail, curry goat, fried red snapper, codfish, and stewed fowl. Rotis are available every day. Vegetarians, beware! We detected pieces of fowl in our *ital* rotis. That aside, the rotis were flavorful, moist, and filling.

THE PUBLIC LOUNGE
Manhattan
210 W. 35th St.
(212) 560-8862
Subway stop: 34th St. on 1, 2, 3, 9, B, D, F, Q, N, or R train

This is a lunch only eatery situated in the rear room of a very old-fashioned bar, also called The Public Lounge. Ignore bar patrons glued to their stools and head for the rear where a Jamaican crew is turning out the best rendition of island food in these parts. Curry chicken, curry goat, jerk chicken, oxtail stew, and "fish cook to order" with a variety of sauces constitute the main bill of fare. Prices range from $4.50 to $7.50 for a platter with two side dishes from a list that includes corn bread, Jamaican style rice and peas, collard greens, macaroni and cheese, white rice, plantains, and green beans. (Order your entrée wrapped in a roti rather than a full-platter deal and pay less.) Bring your own Red Stripe; they don't have it at the bar.

...and a Dominican restaurant:

DALQUIS RESTAURANT

Manhattan
318 W. 36th St. bet. 8th & 9th Aves.
(212) 502-5363
Subway stop: 34th St. on A, C, or E train

The lunch counter in this storefront runs along one wall and ends in a steam table with eight or so main dishes. The steam table entrées–oxtail, pork chops, two kinds of chicken, beefsteak, and codfish salad– are in the $5.00 to $7.50 range and include mounds of rice and beans. Try the codfish salad–three generous spoonfuls of desalinated and rehydrated salt cod, green olives, chopped tomato, green pepper, and Spanish onion dressed with vinegar and olive oil. Chicken baked with garlic and black pepper and strewn with raw onions is also good. Recommended, but not always available, is *pulpo* (octopus) salad. There is a modern jukebox filled with the latest Latin CDs, and decorations include three paintings in Caribbean primitive style, and a copy of Van Gogh's "Sunflowers."

JAPANESE

Whereas only the privileged few can enjoy sushi in Japan, here it is democratized, eaten on nearly every block of the Village by college students and office workers. A rundown of my favorite reasonable downtown places follows:

TASTE OF TOKYO
Manhattan
54 W. 13th St. bet. 5th & 6th Aves.
(212) 691-8666
Subway stop: 14th St. on B, D, F, or Q train

This is a good Japanese restaurant with a neighborhood feel and friendly service.

SAPPORO VILLAGE JAPANESE RESTAURANT
Manhattan
245 E. 10th St. at 1st Ave.
(212) 260-1330
Subway stop: 1st Ave. on L train

This offers the best combination of value and good food. The once innovative menu is now rear guard.

ESASHI

Manhattan
32 Ave. A bet. E. 2nd & 3rd Sts.
(212) 508-8726
Subway stop: 2nd Ave. on F train

This offers excellent early bird specials (until 8:00 P.M.) as cheap as $6.50 as well as above average sushi.

GO

Manhattan
St. Mark's Pl. bet. 2nd & 3rd Aves.
(212) 254-5510
Subway stop: Astor Pl. on 6 train

This restaurant has endeared itself to me by selling hot noodles out on the sidewalk at 2:00 A.M. on the coldest winter mornings.

HAKATA VILLAGE

Manhattan
33 Carmine St. bet. Bleecker & Bedford Sts.
(212) 243-5727
Subway stop: W. 4th St. on A, B, C, D, E, F,
or Q train

This is a branch of the midtown restaurant on West 48th

Street, off the beaten track in an Italian neighborhood. Many offerings are adventuresome, even inspired.

NATORI

Manhattan
158 St. Mark's Pl. bet. 1st & 2nd Aves.
(212) 533-7711
Subway stop: Astor Pl. on 6 train

A postage stamp—size dining room and lengthy waits at peak times notwithstanding, this is one hell of a place.

SHIMA

Manhattan
12 Waverly Pl. bet. Mercer & Greene Sts.
(212) 674-1553
Subway stop: 8th St. on N or R train

One of the downtown Japanese pioneers, this restaurant offers good value. Don't miss the fish pond or the tatami rooms.

In Japan, restaurants serve only one or two specialties—yakitori or tempura or noodles or sushi. Consistent with this, New York City has recently seen the reinvention of the Japanese noodle shop.

TACHIGUI-SOBA

Manhattan
732 7th Ave. bet. W. 48th & 49th Sts.
(212) 265-8181
Subway stop: 49th St. on N or R train

This is one of the best. The bar is on the ground floor of a mirrored duplex space. Upstairs is the seating area, filled with Japanese patrons busy slurping noodles. A bowl of noodles, broth, and chopped green onion, with a cylinder of steamed spinach thrown in, costs $2.79. Each serving of noodles–*udon*, or the heartier buckwheat *soba*–comes precooked in a little plastic tray. The assembler behind the bar adds the noodles to the broth, which is boiling hot and made with *dashi* (a fish-based broth), *mirin* (a sweet wine), and light soy sauce. You may choose items from two menu categories to add to your bowl of noodles. Items in the 93¢ category include potato croquette, shrimp tempura (one quite large shrimp), squid tempura, deep-fried bean curd, and a couple of types of seaweed. Despite the low price, the quantities of these items added to your soup are not skimpy. Items from the $1.86 category include marinated beef, fried chicken, kimchi, and smelt tempura. Side dishes (70¢ to $3.00) include *edamame* (steamed soybeans in pod), *gyoza* (dumplings), chicken rice balls, plain rice balls, and the (untasted) stewed intestines in soybean paste and vegetables. The food is great and the prices are economical.

OISHI NOODLE

Manhattan
1117 6th Ave. at W. 43rd St.
(212) 764-3075
Subway stop: 42nd St. on B, D, F, or Q train

Take this test: Put on your best white shirt and begin to eat the shop's curry *udon* from its quart carryout container. Try to eat all the soup without spattering indelible curry broth on your shirt. (Hint: Keep your face very low to the container.) As you scarf the noodles, note that the soup contains a powerful load of curry powder, lots of *udon*, bok choy, bean sprouts, green onion, slivers of carrot, and more than ten pieces of Chinese barbecued pork. This is a noodle masterpiece. Although the decor is definitely Japanese—with colorful paper lanterns and window curtains that repeat a screened motif of Hokusai's "The Wave"—the food incorporates elements of Chinese cuisine (such as the pork in the curry *udon*). Everything is in the $5.00 to $6.00 price range.

TOKYO LA MEN
Manhattan
90 University Pl. bet. E. 11th & 12th Sts.
(212) 229-1489
Subway stop: Union Sq. on 4, 5, 6, L, N, or R train

This punningly named noodle shop occupies a narrow room with artificial flowers hanging in profusion from the ceiling. Order *ten sin*, inadequately described on the menu as "shrimp, mushroom, *kani* and egg in sweet sauce." The dish is brought in a huge white bowl resting on a round black lacquer tray with one flat side that the server aligns flush with the edge of the table so the bowl is comfortably close for noodle slurping without being off center on the tray. The bowl holds a quart of brown broth complexly flavored and laced with the richness of mushroom and beef. A broad omelet strewn with shredded red ginger and ribbons of spinach floats on top. Excavation beneath the omelet reveals thin noodles, kernels of sweet corn, and tiny pieces of mushroom. Inside the omelet are bits of fake crab (although the menu mentions shrimp, I wasn't sore). Before the noodles are presented, the waiter brings you an appetizer of *inari* sushi, a deep-fried pocket of tofu stuffed with carrot and seaweed-flecked sweet rice. The service is pleasant and attentive.

MENCHANKO-TEI

Manhattan
39 W. 55th St. bet. 5th & 6th Aves.
(212) 247-1585
**Subway stop: 5th Ave. on E or F train; 57th St.
on B or Q train**

Manhattan
131 E. 45th St. bet. 3rd & Lexington Aves.
(212) 986-6805
Subway stop: 42nd St. on 4, 5, or 6 train

This is one of the handful of Japanese restaurants favored mainly by Japanese diners. They don't serve much teriyaki, sushi, or tempura; the menu is centered on rice or noodle soups served in big metal bowls from which you ladle small portions into smaller bowls so that the remainder stays hot. Try the *tokusei guzoni* ($8.50), loaded with chicken, Oriental cabbage, dried mushrooms, sprouts, carrots, Japanese potato, and miraculous gooey islands of rice cake. Save room for the small dishes (around $5.00) that the patrons often share as accompaniments to the soup: crunchy, salty, pickled snow cabbage, Spanish mackerel seasoned with vinegar and sesame seeds, and grilled eel hearts (something of a euphemism for two skewers crammed with sweet, stringy, satisfying eel entrails). If you can, sit in the front room at the eight-seat soup bar. Menchanko-Tei is also noted for its multiple-course

Japanese breakfast, which includes a constellation of small dishes that vary from day to day, priced at $4.75 and $9.75.

SAPPORO

Manhattan
152 W. 49th St. bet. 6th & 7th Aves.
(212) 869-8972
Subway stop: 49th St. on N or R train; 50th St. on 1 or 9 train

Conviently located right off of Times Square, this is another restaurant frequented by Japanese diners. There's a rack of well-thumbed publications from home by the front door with tables separated from a noodle bar by wooden demipartitions. With nary a piece of sushi in sight, the menu is strictly no-nonsense Japanese comfort food. Don't miss the *gyoza* ($4.10), some of the best dumplings in town. Six to a serving, they are stuffed with savory meat and greens, steamed, and then panfried to a crisp brown. Pork and chicken cutlets, served with rice, shredded cabbage, and sweetish *tonkatsu* sauce, are also recommended. This joint is especially cozy in winter, but if you come by during the summer, you can get the pièce de résistance: *hiyashi chuka*, a bowl of cold noodles in a slightly sweet broth, topped with ham, chicken, egg, fish cake, green onion, shredded ginger, cucumber, and corn—a wild and flavorful combo!

KOREAN

Koreans live in a country with hard winters. Perhaps because of the extreme cold, Koreans like food that is hot and spicy and thermally hot as well. Many stews are served from large metal bowls placed over a burning Sterno flame so the stew literally boils as it is eaten. (I put out the Sterno as soon as one of these dishes is served.) The assortment of small dishes, served cold, when you first arrive, can be eaten as appetizers, along with dinner, or after. The most famous of these side dishes—and the centerpiece of Korean cuisine—is kimchi, Chinese cabbage pickled in a solution of vinegar, cayenne, salt, and (sometimes) fish powder. The term also refers to a number of small appetizing dishes that are served at the beginning of the Korean meal. Typical prices at Korean restaurants range from $8.00 to $15.00 per dish—expensive by the standards of this book.

KIM SAS KAS

Queens
38-13 Union St.
(718) 445-1165 and (718) 359-0123
Subway stop: Main St./Flushing on 7 train

Kimchi served on a recent visit were sweet preserved lotus root (which has medicinal properties, our waitress explained), carrot and fried bean curd, mussels in broth, shredded raw beef, and spinach with vinegar and powdered cayenne. Then onto *bulgogi*– a good bet in any Korean eatery. This particular version of razor-shaved beef that you grill at the table included mushrooms and medium-hot long green peppers to be barbecued along with the meat. We also ordered one of those flame-burning-underneath seafood stews: sea cucumber, shrimp, mushrooms, abalone, and seaweed. When I asked the waitress for a translation of five dishes about half the price of the normal ($12.00 or so) entrée, she said they were broth dishes eaten by old men. We tried one–it was perfectly filling, but too bland if you like the hot, hot stuff. It made us feel like old men.

DOE REI

Manhattan
306 5th Ave. bet. E. 31st & 32nd Sts.
(212) 564-8585
Subway stop: 34th St. on B, D, F, Q, N, or R train;
33rd St. on 6 train

A midtown Korean restaurant finally broke the $8.00 to $15.00 price barrier, with a $4.99 special lunch which includes a main dish and many small dishes of Korean vegetables, including various forms of kimchi.

From a choice of four numbered main dishes, *jooke yang* (described on the menu as beef stew) turned out to be a morass of green onions, beef tendon, egg (like in egg drop soup), bean thread vermicelli, and Korean vegetables suspended in a heady red broth thickened with cayenne. (The waitress assured me that numbers 1 and 4 are more suitable for the tender tongued.) Six vegetable side dishes came in addition to the fine main dish, some with two different preparations on a single plate. Shredded daikon radish, tart sautéed zucchini, hard black beans with sesame seeds in sesame oil and corn syrup, and two kinds of Chinese cabbage kimchi. Also provided were a large covered dish of rice and a farewell wedge of refreshing watermelon.

DONG MYUNG OK
(A.K.A. AJUMMA HOUSE)

Manhattan
306 W. 40th St. bet. 8th & 9th Aves.
(212) 695-4080
Subway stop: 42nd St. on A, C, or E train

This is another favorite lumberjack-size lunch for $4.99 at a tiny neighborhood place across from Port Authority. Inside the street scene seems remote. Behind the softly lit bar is a world-class kitsch collection and the hostess periodically comes from behind the bar to offer each patron gum. Wonderful news: She explains that I can have anything on the English menu, in a lunch-size portion, for $4.99–eat in or take out.

After about twenty minutes, I was brought my *deon jang jee gae* to go in a shopping bag weighing over five pounds. Inside, in sturdy reusable plastic containers, was a full quart of pork and pickled vegetable stew with bean curd and delicious, heavy rice noodles in a red broth. (The pork was really pork fat, but the generous quantities of kimchi and bean curd compensated.) In three separate containers were six different side dishes and crinkle-cut rice cake, dyed brown, in a thin sauce garnished with sesame seeds and green onion. There was also a pint of white rice, which is traditionally dumped into the stew after the solid parts have been eaten. Boy, this is worth the wait!

MEXICAN

As recently as ten years ago, good Mexican food was nearly impossible to find in New York City. Most of the Mexican restaurants were shameful purveyors of

slop-on-a-plate. But with the large-scale influx of Mexicans workers over the last decade, the number of first-rate restaurants serving authentic Mexican cuisine has grown. Some favorites are:

PEDRO PARAMO

Manhattan
430 E. 14th St. bet. 1st & 2nd Aves.
(212) 475-4581
Subway stop: 1st Ave. on L train

Since its original opening as a pizza parlor look-alike whose Veracruz owners didn't have a clue about what the public wanted to eat, this place has become more refined, adopted the name of a hero of Mexican literature, and has expanded into an adjacent storefront in response to its spectacular popularity. With entrées priced in the $6.00 to $12.00 range, the menu now concentrates on delicately prepared and presented versions of conventional Mexican dishes, with a few modest innovations, such as burritos stuffed with spicy eggplant or spinach. The enchiladas, refried beans, and rice definitely do not run into each other on the plate here.

EL MAGUEY Y LA TUNA

Brooklyn
533 Grand St. bet. Union Ave. & Lorimer St.
(718) 965-3333
Subway stop: Lorimer St. on L train,
Metropolitan Ave./Grand St. on G train

This capacious restaurant was founded by immigrants from Puebla. At the front of the restaurant is a grill where seven varieties of taco–a large quantity of coarsely chopped beefsteak, lamb, tongue, chorizo, or pork mixed with cilantro in a fresh, oven-warmed corn tortilla–are expertly turned out. At $1.50 apiece, they are quite a bargain. Appetizers are bargains too. *Taquitos al guacamole*–two corn tortillas folded tightly around shredded chicken, deep-fried, and then topped with guacamole, chopped iceberg lettuce, and plenty of grated *queso blanco*–are $2.25. *Camarones ajillo* are five large shrimps sautéed Iberian style with margarine and tons of garlic. At $3.25, how do they do it? Another unbelievable deal: Burritos come two to a plate, for $2.00.

Entrées are generally $5.00 to $6.00, with none priced over $7.00. The *arroz con pollo Mejicana*–t w o chicken drumsticks and a thigh hidden by a mountain of orange rice with corn kernels and carrot chunks–is enormous but a bit bland. Mole *ranchero* is better: The same chicken parts covered in thick savory gravy spiked with hot chiles and chocolate. Other standout entrées are: Pork chops smothered in coarsely chopped canned tomatoes, green peppers and onions, and the chile relleno. All entrées come with rice and refried beans.

LOS MARIACHIS

Brooklyn
805 Coney Island Ave. bet. Cortelyou & Dorchester Rds.
(718) 826-3388
Subway stop: Church Ave. on F, D, or Q train.

Regional dishes that demonstrate both the earthiness and sophistication of Puebla cooking star here. *Guisado de calabasas* features chunks of pork and slices of zucchini that have been slowly stewed in pureed calabash squash. Another fine but expensive choice is *camarones enchilados* ($11.95): five huge shrimp cooked in a fragrant sauce containing julienned green and red bell peppers, onions, garlic, cumin, sweet tomato sauce, and cinnamon.

The house version of shrimp seviche is noteworthy and cheap. For $6.50, you are served an oblong pressed glass dish heaped with raw medium shrimp marinated in lime juice and tossed with finely chopped tomato, onion, cilantro, and jalapeño–all at the peak of freshness in a light spicy-and-sour dressing. Also splendid is the green tamale, whose moist *masa* (cornmeal) interior is studded with long shards of leftover pork, which commingles deliciously with the hot green chile sauce.

RICONCITO MEXICANO
Manhattan
307 W. 39th St. bet. 8th & 9th Aves.
(212) 268-1704
Subway stop: 42nd St. on A, C, or E train

The name of this highly recommended garment center restaurant–also run by Puebla immigrants–ought to be "Rinconcito," which means "little corner" or "little place," but the sign painter omitted one of the *n*'s. Sit at one of the hand-me-down Formica tables surrounded by Mexicans from nearby sweatshops and order one of the two changing main dishes offered at lunch. A $5.00 serving of chicken mole includes rice cooked with chicken fat, refried beans, and five warm tortillas. The mole is made with fresh green poblano chiles, tomatillos, and toasted pumpkin seeds and has an excellent smoky edge. Dense with more flavors than you can identify, it's an authentic peasant dish with no shortcuts taken. Another good choice is fried cheese patties in mole poblano. The chocolate-laced mole poblano is tinged with red oil and tastes tart rather than sweet. The unusual cheese patties, breaded and then deep-fried, taste better than they sound. Tacos are made with diced tongue, beef, chicken, or pork, topped with cilantro and onion, and wrapped in two soft corn tortillas ($1.00). A final note: On Saturdays, El Riconcita makes tamales with freshly ground masa, rather than commercial *masa* harina. They are not to be missed.

MEXICAN FAST FOOD

LA ESPIGA II

Queens
42-13 43rd Ave. bet. Corona & Broadway
(718) 779-7898
Subway stop: Broadway on N train

Printed on the menu of this nifty new Mexican bakery is the slogan: "No solo vendemos pan," which they translate as "We ain't just bread."

In addition to baked goods, La Espiga II also sells Mexican groceries and an extensive menu of snacks: tacos, tamales, and *tortas* (Mexican-style sandwiches made with a crusty roll called a *bolillo*). These sandwiches are available in ten varieties, including *queso de puerco* (head cheese), *chorizo*, *carnitas* (fried pork bits), and *queso amarillo* (American cheese), all dressed with mayonnaise, canned jalapeños, and pieces of avocado, then pressed under a weight on the griddle until warmed through. A ham and cheese sandwich was spicy and excellent. Sauce for the spicy tamales made with chicken and *masa harina* comes inside moist veins of mole *verde*, a green sauce usually made with tomatillos, cilantro, and fresh green chiles. The weekend special is goat steamed in a banana leaf with chiles and salt at $6.50 a pound. Half that quantity is enough for two diners.

DOWNTOWN BAKERY

Manhattan
47 1st Ave. bet. E. 3rd & 4th Sts.
(212) 473-6643
Subway stop: 2nd Ave. on F train

Over a clock featuring a color vignette of "The Last Supper," with the clock hands poking out of Jesus' midsection, the Day-Glo menu board behind the counter lists Mexican specialties in one column and gringo sandwiches in the other. The Mexican selections, all *antojitos* (cornmeal-based snack foods), include tamales, tacos, chimichangas, enchiladas, and quesadillas. The counter lady steered me away from the green sauce and toward the mole poblano (chocolate mole) to go over my chicken enchiladas. Two of these were doused with a pleasantly spicy and sweetish mole, sprinkled with *queso fresca*, and given a finishing zap in the microwave so that the enchiladas were warmed but not cooked. (A small, undressed salad is added to the container post-zap.) At $3.50, this could be one of the best Mexican food deals in town. Other promising selections include avocado salad ($3.25) and *pozole* (hominy soup, $5.75), served with pork tacos and only available on weekends. If you are inclined to eat in, the counter has four bar stools.

FRESCO TORTILLA GRILL

Manhattan
36 Lexington Ave. bet. E. 24th & 25th Sts.
(212) 475-7380
Subway stop: 23rd St. on 6 train

Manhattan
253 8th Ave. bet. W. 22nd & 23rd Sts.
(212) 463-8877
Subway stop: 23rd St. on A, C, or E train

Manhattan
125 W. 42nd St. bet. Broadway & 6th Ave.
(212) 221-5849
Subway stop: Times Sq. on 1, 2, 3, 7, 9, N, R, or S train

FRE$H TORTILLA$
Manhattan
206 Varick St. at Houston St.
(212) 242-3520
Subway stop: Houston St. on I or 9 train

These brethren establishments all look just like Chinese take-out restaurants with light-colored Formica on the counters and walls and Chinese workers. But over the counter, each has a machine, presumably made in Mexico, that forms and fries flour tortillas to order. Like the menu says: "Our Flour Tortilla is made fresh throughout the day, we only bake to your request, to maintain freshness."

Order either the fresh flour tortillas or the quesadillas *sincronizadas*. Notable tortilla stuffers–their relative blandness is an advantage if you acknowledge the primacy of the tortillas–include steak fajita with guacamole, Tex-Mex chile (tastes canned but probably isn't), black bean and cheese, and chicken stew. All are priced $1.29 to $1.99, a tremendous bargain and two make a meal.

When you order your "synchronized" quesadilla, say, the one with cheese and jalapeños, a flour tortilla is pulled from the griddle just as it finishes cooking and then put on another griddle where it is topped with lots of Monterey Jack cheese, jalapeños, and another fresh tortilla. "Fresh" is inadequate to describe these tortillas: They are pre-fresh. Don't bother with the hard-shell tacos–they're store-bought. Buy the flour tortillas instead, then take them home and stuff them yourself.

VALLE OF MEXICO AZTECA GROCERY

Brooklyn
160 Bedford Ave. bet. Grand Ave. & N. First St.
(718) 599-1200
Subway stop: Bedford Ave. on L train

This pocket-sized store, that carries a broad range of products needed for making Mexican food, comes alive each day at 4:00 P.M. when a counter is pushed onto the sidewalk and they begin making tacos. Choices are chicken or pork, chopped on a cutting board made from a section of tree trunk, and heated on a griddle fired with bottled gas. The tacos, as is customary, are prepared with two soft corn tortillas, freshly made nearby at the Tortilleria Piaxtla (613 Flushing Avenue). Their glory lies in the array of sauces and other taco toppers, including kidney beans stewed with onion, pickled jalapeños, and fresh salsa made from ripe tomatoes, cilantro, and onion. Additional sauces and guacamole, as well as the red and green moles, are all made from scratch. The red mole, still warm when I put some on my pork taco, is brick red, spicy, and complex with a slightly nutty edge. The green mole is mainly tomatillos, cilantro, and jalapeño chiles. The thick, lump-free, very garlicky guacamole is poured over ice cubes in a bowl to keep it from getting brown.

TACO STAND
Manhattan
Corner of W. 48th St. & 9th Ave.
Subway stop: 50th St. on C train

These are simply the best tacos in the city. The stand, open after 6:00 P.M., seven nights a week, consists of a table like you might find in a church basement. A glass case on top holds seven plastic bowls of taco toppings: mole verde, chopped purple onions, pico de gallo, hot red chile sauce, pinto beans, sliced radishes, and shredded lettuce. At the right, a surreal device that looks like an inverted wok is used to warm tortillas. Around the base of the dome runs a broad trough, mounded with taco fillings: chopped sausage, ground beef, chopped pork, shredded chicken, and cubed potatoes cooked with glistening pieces of spicy green serrano chile. For $2.00, the proprietor will pile your taco as high as the Styrofoam plate allows with any combination of the good-looking ingredients. When my host offered to put "a little of everything" on, I readily accepted. With its stray beans and creamy potato pieces melding nicely into the multiple meats, it was so good, I immediately had another made the same way.

TAMALE LADIES

Manhattan
8th Ave. bet. W. 38th & 40th Sts.
Subway stop: 42nd St. on A, C, or E train

On a chilly November evening around the time when office workers stream by, bound for their Port Authority buses, two tamale vendors appear. The first, between 38th and 39th Streets, was accompanied by her husband, who looks out nervously for cops and makes change. Inside a wire shopping cart, a towel-nested, foil-lined aluminum pot holds twenty or so steaming tamales wrapped in corn husks. The tamales are $1 apiece, a price that prevails with every vendor. My half foot-long prize was a thick flattened cylinder of cornmeal mush containing plenty of finely crushed black pepper. A line of frayed chunks of beef ran down the center. The fat from the beef melted into the cornmeal. Delicious! Another time, the cornmeal mush was spicy and red from lacings of red pepper. (The filling might have been pork, but, frankly, I'm not sure what it was.)

The second tamale vendor, between 39th and 40th Streets with no lookout, had chicken tamales–not quite so good, but less greasy. These were also wrapped in corn husks, held together with a neat bow made from a strip of husk. You can also purchase these tamales in bulk from both ladies, refrigerate them, and resteam them at home.

MIDDLE EASTERN

Much of the Middle East, including Syria, Israel, Jordan, Lebanon, and Egypt, was part of the Ottoman Empire for the six centuries preceding our own. The Ottoman legacy can be seen in the common culinary heritage of these countries, most obviously in the small dishes often served at lunch or as appetizers: hummus, falafel, tabbouleh, and *babaganouj* (the spelling of these varies wildly). These dishes, which can be found in any Middle Eastern restaurant and in Turkish and Greek ones as well, are tasty and have the added advantage of being good for you. But if you've become familiar enough with them to be on the verge of boredom, look beyond the section of the menu designated as *maza* or meze, and search out those dishes that differentiate the cuisines of the Middle East rather than unite them. Some places to begin your search are:

VILLAGE CROWN

Manhattan
96 3rd Ave. bet. E. 12th & 13th Sts.
(212) 674-2061
Subway stop: 3rd Ave. on L train

The dining room of this recently opened kosher Israeli restaurant is done in shades of blue and green with Plexiglas clouds hanging from the ceiling and a colorful mural of Jerusalem painted on the wall. In addition to the standard menu of tabbouleh, *babaganouj*, hummus, and unusually distinguished falafel (each about $4), the menu has sections. The most interesting is devoted to the Sephardic cuisine of Morocco and Yemen. Moroccan specialties ($8.95 to $12.95) include couscous in four varieties–lamb, vegetable, meat, and chicken–and *tajin* of chicken, boneless chicken, raisins, and eggplant in a thick stew, with rice and salad on the side. Good appetizers are mushroom *kuba*, a deep-fried dumpling with a cracked outside and sweet mushroom filling, and a superb purse of phyllo dough stuffed with pureed chickpeas called *sumbusak* (both $3.95).

HUDSON FALAFEL

Manhattan
516 Hudson St. bet. Christopher & W. 10th Sts.
(212) 242-3939
Subway stop: Christopher St. on 1 or 9 train

The vegetarian combo ($5.50) comes in a compartmentalized white Styrofoam tray and includes tabbouleh, *babaganouj*, Greek salad with feta cheese, two fried-to-order falafel, a pair of Italian hot peppers, three dill pickle slices, a pile of shredded lettuce and another of chopped tomatoes, fava bean salad, onion and parsley relish, cumin-laced hummus, a cup of tahini dressing, and a pita bread. Whew! When I get this special (about once a week), I usually share it with one or even two people it's so big. This hole-in-the-wall eatery, decorated by its Jordanian proprietors with verses from the Koran, is a boon to vegetarians, the health-conscious, and the budgetwise. The glass case next to the French doors often contains Middle Eastern dishes you won't find in other places. Don't miss pumpkin kibbe, a deep-fried and ocarina-shaped dumpling with a pumpkin-and-cracked wheat shell filled with a mixture of slightly sour spinach, chickpeas and walnuts–absolutely delicious. Meat is also offered: The gyro is good, the lamb kebab and chicken kebabs so-so. Some good, weird sodas have names like Wink (grapefruit) and Cactus Cooler (orange-pineapple).

MOUSTACHE

Manhattan
90 Bedford St. bet. Grove & Barrow Sts.
(212) 229-2220
Subway stop: Christopher St. on 1 or 9 train

The specialty of this sunny, appealing Iraqui-owned restaurant is freshly baked pita, which comes out of a pizza oven steaming and extravagantly inflated. Costing $1.00, the pita must be eaten within five minutes or it turns into the dry, flat variety you buy in the supermarket. Moustache uses these pitas hot out of the oven to make sandwiches such as the one made with the cumin-laced lamb *merguez* ($6.00). They also use the pita dough to make "pitza," their name for a pita pizza. These are about eight inches in diameter and the deep brown crust–a little more brittle and oily than regular pizza crust–is topped with cheese and tomato sauce ($6.00). Optional ingredients, such as capers, olives, eggplant, artichokes, or mushrooms, cost $1.00 each. A particularly appealing choice is garlic and parsley. The best thing in the place is zatter bread, a pita topped with loads of thyme and sprinkled with sesame seeds and olive oil ($4.00). Another delicious surprise are the beverages, including loomi, a tart lemonade, and ayran, a yogurt drink.

SOUTH AMERICAN

Who invented seviche? Where did the chile pepper originate? What's an arepa? These are the sorts of questions you'll be asking yourself as you explore the newest and most exciting category of New York ethnic food, South American. The restaurants surveyed here feature the very distinctive cuisines of Colombia, Chile, Ecuador, Brazil, and Peru. To really get a feel for South American cooking, you'll have to try them all.

COSTAL COLUMBIANA

Queens
21-20 35th Ave. at 42nd St.
(718) 706-0663
Subway stop: Steinway on G or R train

Costal Columbiana offers a broad selection of fish, beef, and chicken dishes, plus a pair of special stews each day (medium bowl, $4.00; large, $5.00). My medium order of the Latin American tripe stew called *mondongo* came in a cereal bowl—size portion. The broth–green with cilantro, smelling intensely of garlic–contained ragged pieces of tripe and an equal number of chunks of good pork. Potatoes, peas, carrots, and rice filled out the bowl. This was the best version of the dish I've ever tasted, and the addition of pork prevented the tripe from becoming tiresome or cloying. The chorizo appetizer ($3.50) brought me one large, garlicky sausage, garnished with onion, tomato, and lettuce, plus an *arepa*. (*Arepas* are small cakes made from cornmeal mush that have been boiled, baked, and then reheated on a grill, which leaves charred hash marks on the top and bottom. Hard as rocks outside, *arepas* are white and fluffy inside. They are eaten split and spread with margarine.) It's quite a plate of food.

POMAIRE

Manhattan
371 W. 46th St. bet. 8th & 9th Aves.
(212) 456-3055
Subway stop: 42nd St. on A, C, or E train

Pomaire is a quiet Chilean village not far from Santiago that is famous for its pottery. Pomaire's design evokes the town with a great display of pottery.

First, the waiter brings to your table bread, butter,

and a small clay pot of salsa with a tiny spoon. The bread, still warm, comes in small round loaves, flat like Moroccan bread. It's delicious and can be smeared with butter or, even better, the red salsa tasting of onion, garlic, and cilantro, all married by olive oil. From the Special Menu—eight entrées that come with salad, dessert, and coffee for $12.95—I went for *pastel de choclo y ensalada chilena*, a casserole based on corn puree that contains ground beef, chopped chicken, sliced egg, pitted black olives, and onions baked in a brown crock with sugar sprinkled on top. The rich, intensely corny sweetness is unusual and appreciated. *Pollo arvejard*, sampled from the regular dinner menu, turned out to be a large half chicken with a nondescript sauce and lots of boiled peas and carrots—wholesome but not exotic. Carbo alert: It comes with both rice and deep-fried potato cubes.

CABANA CARIOCA

Manhattan
123 W. 45th St. bet. 6th Ave. & Broadway
(212) 581-8088
Subway stop: 42nd St. on 1, 2, 3, 7, 9, N, R, or S train

Brazilian food is not easy to come by in New York, and when you find it, it's usually dull. The zestiest is found at Coffee Shop on Union Square, but only a small percentage of the menu is Brazilian. This venerable joint east of Times Square, famous for its lunch buffet, is my second choice. The ground floor dining room–warmly lit and decorated with colorful murals, hanging wicker baskets, and exposed brick–offers an $8.95 buffet that features twenty-two items on a long skirted steam table. My favorite is a salt cod, onion, and potato casserole, with buttery kale a close second. *Feijoada*, the national dish of Brazil, suffers from being underdone. Other steam table offerings are roast pork with gravy, razor-thin, deep-fried pork cutlet, baked chicken, fried calamari, cold microshrimp salad, red beans, well-oiled white rice, french-fried potato slices, and potato salad with ham. Best of the seven dessert items is a terrific creme caramel.

The buffet on the utilitarian third floor is $4.95. With only eight selections, its steam table is a pale shadow of the downstairs installation. Still, the wonderful salt cod casserole was there, and so too was the good roasted chicken. I cast my vote for upstairs.

INTI RAYMI

Queens
86-14 37th Ave. bet. 86th & 87th Sts.
(718) 424-1938
Subway stop: 90th St. on 7 train

Named for the king of the Inca gods, Inti Raymi is the king of New York Peruvian restaurants, offering a variety of dishes that reflect the culinary heritage of

the Incas–potatoes, corn, hot peppers, and cheese–
rather than the international Hispanic cuisine which
can be found in many other restaurants.

Much of the food here is spicy hot (hot peppers
may have originated in Peru or neighboring
Ecuador). With Ecuador and Mexico right behind,
Peru also claims the invention of seviche. *Ceviche de
mariscos* ($10.75) contains enough shrimp, octopus,
scallops, clams, conch, and fish "cooked" in lemon
juice to serve four as an appetizer, two as an entrée.
Papa a la Huancaina ($4.25) is an appetizer of cold
potatoes with a spicy cheese sauce, which can also
be enjoyed with a steak ($9.25). *Aji de gallina* ($5.25)
is shredded chicken in a spicy sauce thickened with
bread. Don't miss *chicha morada*, a delicious fruit
beverage made with pineapple and lemon, flavored
with cloves, and colored with purple corn.

The menu demonstrates how Peruvians have
incorporated Italian and Cantonese dishes into their
national menu. An example is *tallarin saltado de
camarones* (lo mein with shrimp), which was introduced to Peru by Chinese immigrants in the 1920s.
This is a restaurant where everyone can find something to love.

THAI

The food at Thai restaurants in New York City is often priced at three to four dollars more per dish than a similar quantity of Chinese food. We are told this is not the case on the West Coast, where Thai food is more common and priced on a par with Chinese food. Three Thai restaurants that break the price barrier, with appealing results, are:

THAI CAFE

Brooklyn
925 Manhattan Ave. at Kent St.
(718) 383-3562
Subway stop: Greenpoint Ave. on G train

This cafe in the mainly Polish Greenpoint section of Brooklyn has five tables, a counter with five stools, and no kitchen. All dishes are prepared at the stove and grill behind the counter, almost under your nose. Two cooks work furiously, turning out dishes with military precision. All food is strictly made to order.

At only $2.50, the squid salad appetizer–tender squid mixed with shredded iceberg lettuce, cilantro, cucumber, tomato, scallions, onions, and julienned carrots in a fiery-sweet chili dressing–is large enough for lunch. *Pad thai* ($4.25) is a mixture of rice stick noodles, grilled shrimp, scallions, and tiny chunks of dried bean curd film with an agreeable heap of bean sprouts on top. Sliced chicken with bamboo shoots and basil in coconut curry sauce is exactly what it says, but this doesn't hint at the transcendent orange color of the sauce in the serving bowl. With a similar concern for display, a grilled shrimp salad containing tomato, onion, scallion, and cucumber is flanked by a haystack of grated purple cabbage. The beef with zucchini in a dark peanut sauce is set off by a precise array of cucumber slices.

All of the nearly fifty menu items are priced from $4.00 to $7.95 and could serve as dinner entrées. Most are Thai, with some odd exceptions: beef burrito, shrimp and vegetable tempura, egg fettuccine with seafood marinara, and fish and chips.

KUN PAW

Manhattan
39 Greenwich Ave. at Charles St.
(212) 989-4100
Subway stop: W. 4th St. on A, B, C, D, E, F, or Q train

Giant picture windows looking out on two sides give the dining room an airy feeling. Riffing on a familiar list of ingredients, the kitchen comes up with some pleasing new combinations. Try *kow soy* ($6.95), presented in a handled crock and something of an architectural wonder. The crock is filled with a thin sauce of coconut milk and red curry paste. Below the curry line is a patty of fried noodles, topped with sprouts, green beans, chicken, broccoli, carrots, and celery. So far, so good, but what really makes this dish is the sprinkling of sour bok choy. Wrinkled green pieces of pickled Chinese cabbage provide the primary flavor challenge to the curry. Two eating hints: Ask for extra sour cabbage; as soon as the dish arrives, dredge some noodles out of the sauce and position them so they stay crisp. (This helps maintain the pleasant riot of textures.) Appetizers ($3.50 to $4.95) are a particularly good deal, and the menu offers plenty of vegetarian dishes. Final hint: The peanut sauce is better than the tamarind.

RUNGSIT

Manhattan
161 E. 23rd St. bet. Lexington & 3rd Aves.
(212) 260-0704
Subway stop: 23rd St. on 6 train

A friend who was in the Peace Corps in Thailand pronounced this place an authentic Thai establishment. Although the kitchen does a great job on all the traditional Thai dishes, its real strength is noodles. *Pad thai* here is sensational—flavorful and not greasy. The small portion ($5.25) is a substantial entrée for one diner; the large ($7.75) feeds a table. Seven other noodle dishes include *spaghetti kee maow* (stir-fried with baby shrimp, chicken, onion, scallions, basil, and chili) and *pad macaroni* (stir-fried with chicken, egg, onion, scallions, and tomato sauce).

Then there are the noodle soups. My favorite is the seafood noodle soup, a big bowl filled with delicious broth, rice noodles, shrimp, squid, "crabmeat," fish balls, and fried fish cake. I haven't tried the house noodle soup, which is billed as "a spicy combination of meat balls, beef stew, beef tendon, beef tripes, and sliced of beef." Perhaps next time. (E.M.)

TURKISH

For me, a Turkish meal usually involves a large selection of appetizers (meze) followed by a couple of different grilled kebabs. Common vegetable-based meze typically served at room temperature include *imam bayildi* (eggplant stuffed with tomatoes, onions, and garlic), *patlican salatasi* (roasted eggplant pureed with garlic), dolma (grape leaves stuffed with any number of fillings, almost always including rice), and *boureks* (cigarette-shaped filled phyllo turnovers).

I've ranked the following list of Turkish restaurants in order of preference, with high marks going to places that make their own bread, give especially big portions for the money, or have a larger than usual range of dishes available. Unless otherwise mentioned, decor is acceptably nondescript.

BEYTI KEBAB
Union City, New Jersey
4105 Park Ave. at Pathmark St.
(201) 865-6281

When twenty of us celebrated a birthday here, our ravenous party ate plate after plate of meze and mixed kebabs piled high on platters, and drank glass after glass of raki for a bargain price of less than $20.00 per person. The hummus was the best I've ever tasted, coarsely textured but light, with a restrained touch to the garlic. It's served with fine Turkish bread, a round, yeasty loaf with a wrinkled brown crust and resilient white interior. Someone with a more moderate appetite is likely to get by for $10.00 or so. Chicken shish kebabs, marinated in yogurt and moister than most, are especially good. Don't miss *kisir*, a salad of bulgur with a thick, peppery tomato dressing.

TACI'S BEYTI

Brooklyn
1955 Coney Island Ave. near Kings Hwy.
(718) 627-5750
Subway stop: Kings Hwy. on D, F, or Q train

The knockout here is *yogurtlu adana kebab*, cylinders of lamb chopped with sweet red peppers and hot chiles sitting in a thick yogurt sauce that has been poured over hunks of toasted pita. The yogurt has a touch of tomato sauce in it and the pita has been dipped in butter. Other pluses are generous servings and a better-than-average meze list. My favorites here are *patlican kizartmasi*, deep-fried slices of eggplant with a garlicky yogurt sauce, and oversize *yalanci dolma*, grape leaves stuffed with rice and pine nuts–delicious and freshly made. The biggest bummer is the commercial pita served as table bread.

SAHARA PALACE

Brooklyn
2337 Coney Island Ave. near Ave. U
(718) 376-8594
Subway stop: Ave. U on D or F train

Disregard the desolate location. Even if the food here wasn't first-rate, the fact that this place bakes its own bread would be enough to make you check it out. The bread is an oblong loaf, sprinkled with both yellow and black sesame seeds, brown, flat, and crusty. The interior is white, porous, resilient–perfect bread, fit to be compared with any bread on earth, especially with the excellent meze. *Arnavut cigeri* ($5.00) is cubes of baby calves liver that have been dusted with flour and sautéed in paprika-laced oil. The version of *patlican salatasi* ($3.00) varies the usual plainish puree of eggplant and garlic with small cubes of tomato and sweet red pepper.

After going through many plates of meze and much of the generous bread basket, our threesome had room for only one main course. We chose the mixed grill ($14.95), with four different preparations of lamb: *doner* kebab, shish kebab, lamb chops, and for the *adana* kebab., we asked to substitute *beyti* kebab because it contains chopped red chile and lots more garlic. Both of the last two kebabs are a matter of pride for most Turkish restaurants. The coarsely chopped lamb they're made from requires a special technique–two sharp swords wielded simultaneously, one in each hand.

ALI BABA

Manhattan
245 W. 38th St. bet. 7th & 8th Aves.
(212) 764-2873
Subway stop: 34th St. on 1, 2, 3, 9, A, C, or E train

This garment center favorite is extremely inexpensive. Head for the long glass case of salad components. At least two or three of the daily lineup are distinctly Turkish meze. (Although *imam bayildi* here is ho-hum, don't miss the deep-fried eggplant slices or the grilled vegetables on top of the case.) The best thing to do: Assemble a salad from the many choices and add a kebab or two. (If you ignore the overhead menu, kebabs may be ordered individually.)

VIETNAMESE

Until a couple of years ago, there were only two Vietnamese restaurants that I knew of in the city, and both were considerably more expensive than Chinese restaurants serving food of similar quality. Nowadays, Vietnamese food is more common, and many Vietnamese restaurants undercut Chinese restaurants in price. You can often have a full meal for less than $5.00 and enjoy an assortment of meats over rice with the sweet-and-sour sauce that is one of the hallmarks of Vietnamese cuisine. Other specialties include ground shrimp on a piece of sugarcane and excellent spring rolls, which come with lettuce and fresh mint leaves. And you no longer have to go to Manhattan's Chinatown.

GIA LAM

Brooklyn
5402 8th Ave. bet. 54th & 55th Sts.
(718) 854-8818
Subway stop: 53rd St. on N or R train

At the southern end of Brooklyn's Chinatown in Sunset Park, this Vietnamese restaurant is often thronged with Vietnamese families eating spring rolls and bowls of soup with rice stick noodles. One such soup is pho dac biet ($4.25), described on the menu as "special rice noodles soup w. beef, brisket, navel, flank & tendon." To the uninitiated, these various forms of beef are indistinguishable. But to the Vietnamese, each has a unique character and they are mixed and matched in eight different soups, and in a number of entrées as well. The soup, made with a thin but flavorful meat broth, contains flat rice noodles and a sprinkling of chopped scallions. It is served with a plate of sprouts and fresh basil leaves that can be mixed with the soup, eaten by themselves between bites, or applied to anything else you order.

The excellent and unusually large spring rolls contain ground pork and vermicelli wrapped in superthin rice paper. A small plate with romaine lettuce leaves and fresh mint leaves comes on the side. (I thought that you were supposed to wrap each roll in a leaf with some mint before downing it, but Vietnamese diners nearby wolfed them down straight and reserved the lettuce for bites between mouthfuls of soup.)

One of the best things here is *goi tom can tay* ($5.00), a delicious and plentiful cold salad of boiled shrimp and crisp celery dressed with vinegar and crushed roasted peanuts. It leaves you wondering how they can afford to give you so many shrimp at that price. We rounded out our luncheon with *com suon bi cha tom* ($4.50), an unusual and inexpensive over-rice selection that includes a hot grilled pork chop, cold shredded roast pork, and a weird egg/shrimp/vermicelli pancake. I use the dish, available in every Vietnamese coffee shop, as a benchmark to make an immediate appraisal of the joint. It's okay here, but not up to the highest standard. Nevertheless, this is one of the overall best and most pleasant Vietnamese eateries around.

LITTLE SAIGON CAFE
Manhattan
374 W. 46th St. near 9th Ave.
(212) 956-0639
Subway stop: 42nd St. on A, C, or E train; 49th St. on N or R train

When they say little, they mean little. This cafe in the theater district's self-proclaimed Restaurant Row has only twelve seats at four tables and a kitchen so small that you couldn't lie down in it. But the dining room is cheerful, with a total lack of pretense, and the food is quite a bargain: No dish is over $6.25, and most of the noodle soup and over-rice selections are priced around $4.25.

Quantities are generous: Vietnamese-style beef noodle soup is a full quart of noodles and thinly sliced beef in a substantial broth seasoned with onions, lemongrass, and fresh whole mint leaves. It comes with a little cup of fish sauce mixed with hot pepper sauce, which can be added to the soup. Vietnamese-style fried rice is oily, red, and slightly spicy, with pieces of shrimp and chicken. The highlight of the meal is the chef's special *kim-ting* shrimp ($6.25) from the higher priced end of the menu. Six good-sized shrimp are wrapped in rice paper and stuffed with vermicelli and ground pork–it's like a shrimp shoved into a spring roll. The usual sweet vinegar dipping sauce has a dash of fish sauce, an outstanding addition. End your meal with "French Black Condensed Milk Coffee" or one of the other slow-dripping varieties made at your table. During the summer, the cafe puts a couple of tables out on the sidewalk.